Praise for
The Bible Unlocked

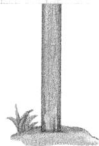

"The lessons are extremely well-written and easy to understand. As a mom of five children, ages preschool to high school, I highly recommend this resource for parents, caregivers, or teachers who long to engage children with the truth, beauty, and wonder of God's Word."
~Heather Platt, wife of David Platt, bestselling author of *Radical*

"I love, love, love this book! My son prefers this book to other Bible books we've tried, and we've tried many. The material is presented in a fun, multi-sensory way."
~Miranda, pastor's wife and mother of two

"I cannot praise this book enough! The material is thorough and fun with each story containing a timeline of events and map work. What engaging discussion my daughter and I have enjoyed as we've worked through the text learning together!"
~Emily, pastor's wife and mother of four

"The Bible really came to life for my daughter. I would recommend this book to anyone who wants their children to know God and His love for them."
~Anne, mother of three

"It's a fun, interactive curriculum that my daughter loved. It's helped her to understand God and know Him better. Her relationship with Jesus has grown a lot. We are so thankful to have found this."
~Kiristin, mother of four

FROM KIDS:

"It's so fun and it makes the Bible fun!"
~7-year-old

"I love learning Bible geography!"
~6-year-old

"This is the best Bible program I've come across. It's fun, unique, informative, and engaging—and it actually works! The lessons are easy to follow, but they make you think. Often with Bible programs you get one or the other—fun or informative—but this one is both! I have a much better understanding of the Bible. This was a great experience and I highly recommend it."
~13-year-old

To the greatest generation yet!
May you unlock all God's
dreams for you.

Printed in the United States of America

Published by MBM Media Press
mbmmedia.org

ISBN (paperback, color): 979-8-9872596-0-3
ISBN (paperback, black/white): 979-8-9872596-1-0
ISBN (e-book): 979-8-9872596-2-7

The Bible Unlocked

What Every Kid Should Know

Master the Bible Ministries

MBM Media Press

Contents

New Testament

Old Testament

Introduction

How do we help our children become everything God's dreamed for them? The key lies in knowing and experiencing the Bible—God's personal revelation of himself to humanity.

The Bible Unlocked isn't just an adventure through the Bible. It's an invitation to experience the Bible personally while mastering its main people, places, events, and teachings. With this book you can:

- Experience the Bible in interactive readings that bring the stories to life
- Learn the most-mentioned places in the Bible in easy steps
- Learn a timeline of Bible events in order
- Meet the most-mentioned people in the Bible
- Unlock deep meaning in thought-provoking questions

The book is designed around research into how the brain learns best. That means you should be able to learn more about the Bible faster and remember it longer.

Our goal is to take you beyond knowing what the Bible says, past understanding what it means. We aim to connect you with the One who inspired the Bible. May you and your family discover his beauty, feel his love, and open his plans for your life. May each chapter hold a treasure just for you that God himself unlocks.

Online Resources

You'll find links to the printable maps, music, games, and the free Kingdom Keys app at:

MBMmedia.org

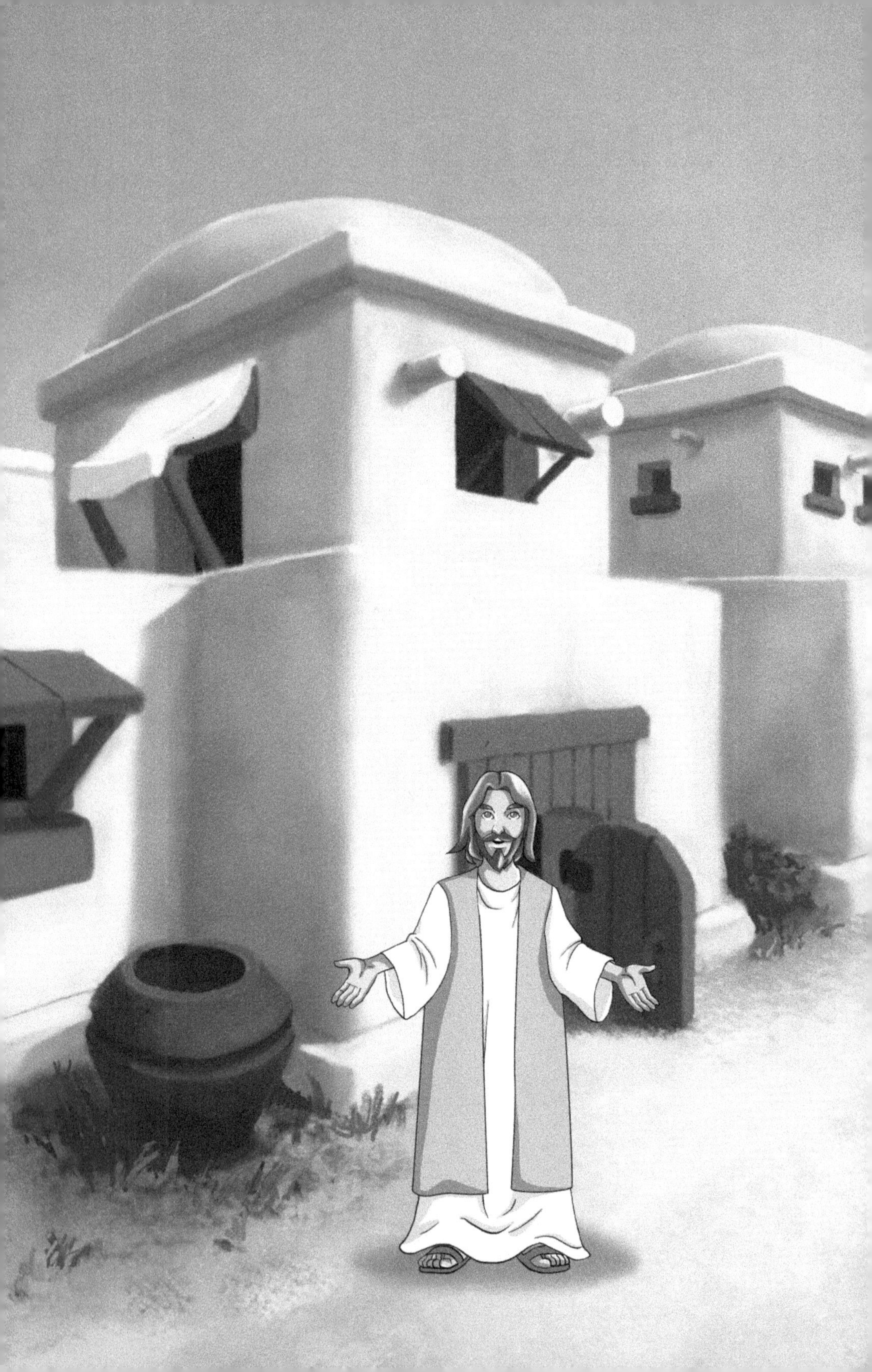

New Testament

The Savior

~

The Church

~

The Teachings

CHAPTER 1

Jesus Starts Out

Luke 1-2, Mark 4, John 3

DIRECTIONS: Read the story to yourself. Or read it as a family with each person reading a different part aloud. When you come to a place name in **bold**, draw a dove in that location on a map in Appendix E.

Jesus is Born
Luke 1-2

NARRATOR: God sent an angel named Gabriel to **Nazareth**, a town in the region of **Galilee**. Gabriel came to a virgin who had promised to marry a man named Joseph. Joseph was a descendent of Israel's King David. The virgin's name was Mary.

Mary

Mary is the mother of Jesus. She believed she would give birth to Jesus even though it was impossible. That's what faith is—believing what God says. Every time we believe God, we give power to what God wants to happen in our lives.

GABRIEL: Hello to the one God favors! The Lord is with you. God has blessed you among women!

NARRATOR: When Mary saw the angel, she was very troubled and began thinking about what this greeting could mean.

GABRIEL: Don't be afraid, Mary. God is very pleased with you. You will become pregnant and give birth to a son. You will name him Jesus. He will be great and will be called the Son of the Most High. The Lord God will make him king like his father David long ago. He will rule over Israel forever, and there will be no end to his Kingdom.

MARY: How can this happen since I am a virgin?

GABRIEL: The Holy Spirit will come on you, and the power of the Most High will cover you. The Holy One that will be born will be called the Son of God. Your relative Elizabeth, who is old, is going to have a baby, too. People had said she couldn't be a mother. But she's already in her sixth month of pregnancy. For nothing spoken by God is impossible.

MARY: I am the servant of the Lord. Let everything you said happen to me.

Jesus is Baptized and Teaches Mark 1, John 3

NARRATOR: Mary gave birth to Jesus just like the angel said. When Jesus was about thirty years old, his cousin John—the son of Elizabeth—was a famous prophet. Listen to what John was preaching.

JOHN: Turn away from your sins! The kingdom of God is near to you!

NARRATOR: Everyone in **Judea** and **Jerusalem** went out to him. He baptized them in the **Jordan River** after they confessed their sins. John was clothed with camel's hair, and he wore a leather belt around his waist. He ate locusts and wild honey. He preached:

JOHN: After me someone will come who is greater than I am. I'm not worthy to even bend down and untie his sandals. I baptized you in water, but he will baptize you in the Holy Spirit. God wants to make it clear to you who this person is. That's why I came baptizing with water.

NARRATOR: One day Jesus came from Nazareth of Galilee and was baptized by John in the Jordan. As he came up from the water, he saw the heavens parting, and the Spirit

John the Baptist

Is this Jesus' cousin John or the prophet Elijah? John the Baptist came with the anointing of Elijah (and his taste in clothes) to prepare the way for Jesus. Jesus called John the greatest prophet in the Bible. When people turned away from their sins, John baptized them. He helped people focus their hearts on God so that they'd be ready to meet Jesus.

descending on him like a dove. A voice came out of the sky:

GOD'S VOICE: You are my Son, whom I love so much. I'm very pleased with you.

NARRATOR: After Jesus was baptized, he began working for God. The first teaching he gave that's recorded in the Bible is his conversation with a religious leader named Nicodemus. Coming to Jesus in **Jerusalem** at night, Nicodemus said:

NICODEMUS: Rabbi, we know that you are a teacher come from God because no one can do these signs that you do unless God is with him.

JESUS: You can be sure what I'm about to tell you is true. A person has to be born again to see God's kingdom.

Preparing for the Mission

When Jesus was a child, he spent years studying the Bible to prepare for God's plan for his life (Luke 2:46). Now he needed one more thing. Before he began his mission, Jesus was baptized. That's when he received power from God's Holy Spirit (Acts 10:38). To live God's plan for our lives, we need to know the Bible and be filled with God's Spirit—just like Jesus.

NICODEMUS: How can I be born when I'm old? Can I go into my mother's womb again and be born?

JESUS: A person has to be born of water and spirit to enter God's Kingdom! When people are born from a person, their bodies are alive. But when people are born from God's Spirit, their spirits are alive. Don't be surprised that I told you, "You have to be born again."

NICODEMUS: How can this be?

JESUS: Are you the teacher of Israel and don't understand these things? No one has gone up into heaven except for the one who came down from heaven. He is the Son of Man. Whoever believes in him will live forever with God. For God loved the world so much that he gave his one and only Son. Anyone who believes in him will not die but will have eternal life. For God didn't send his Son into the world to judge the world. But he sent him so that the world would be saved through him.

Review It!

Which angel spoke to Mary? What did he tell her?

Where was John baptizing people?

What happened after John baptized Jesus?

What did Jesus tell Nicodemus he must do to see God's kingdom?

Remember It!

SONG: *What did Jesus do in the Beginning?*

Learn these timeline events.

1. Baptized by John the Baptist
2. Tempted in the Wilderness
3. First disciples follow him
4. Wedding in Cana—first Miracle
5. Cleanses the Temple
6. Tells Nicodemus how to see God's Kingdom

Why does it matter that Jesus was born to a virgin?

Why did Jesus start his ministry by being baptized rather than by preaching a sermon or doing a miracle?

What did Jesus mean when he told Nicodemus he had to be born again?

I can't get to heaven by doing good things.
I must trust in God's Savior.

Map It!

Dots show where cities are. Lines show where regions are. Label these places:

- Nazareth
- Bethlehem
- Cana
- Jerusalem
- Jordan River

Answers in Appendix E Map 1

CHAPTER 2

Miracles

Matthew 8, Luke 8

DIRECTIONS: Read the story to yourself. Or read it as a family with each person reading a different part aloud. When you come to a place name in **bold**, draw a boat in that location on a map in Appendix E.

One Day of Miracles — Matthew 8

NARRATOR: Jesus did so many miracles that if we tried to write them all down, the world wouldn't have room for all the books that would be written. So, we'll look at what Jesus did on just one day to give us a picture of what every day was like with Jesus.

When Jesus came down from the mountain, a large crowd followed him. A man with a skin disease came to him and worshiped him.

MAN WITH SKIN DISEASE: Lord, if you want to, you can make me clean.

NARRATOR: Jesus stretched out his hand and touched him, saying:

JESUS: I want to. Be made clean.

NARRATOR: Immediately his skin disease was gone.

JESUS: Don't tell anybody. But go and show your clean skin to the priests. Then offer the gift that Moses commanded to let them know that you're healed.

Gift

Jesus never asked someone if they were good enough to be helped or if they deserved to be healed. Having Jesus help us isn't something we earn or deserve. It's a free gift from God.

NARRATOR: When he came into **Capernaum**, a centurion soldier came to him.

SOLDIER: Lord, my servant is lying in my house, and he can't move. He's in a lot of pain.

JESUS: I will come and heal him.

SOLDIER: Lord, I'm not good enough for you to come to my house. Just say what needs to happen, and my servant will be healed. I am also a man under authority with soldiers under my command. I tell this one, "Go," and he goes. I tell another, "Come," and he comes. And I tell my servant, "Do this," and he does it.

NARRATOR: When Jesus heard it, he was amazed. To the crowd Jesus said:

JESUS: What I'm about to tell you is true. I haven't found anyone who has such a great faith in Israel. Many people will come from the east and the west and will sit down with Abraham, Isaac, and Jacob in the Kingdom of Heaven. But some people think they are part of the Kingdom because of the family into which they were born. These people will be thrown out into the outer darkness. There will be weeping and gnashing of teeth.

NARRATOR: To the centurion, Jesus said:

JESUS: You can go. It will be done for you just as you believed.

NARRATOR: His servant was healed that hour.

When Jesus came into Peter's house, he saw Peter's mother-in-law lying down sick with a fever. He touched her hand, and the fever left her. She got up and served him. When evening came, the disciples brought to him many people who were controlled by evil spirits. He cast out the spirits with a word, and he healed all who were sick. He was fulfilling a prophecy given by Isaiah, which said:

ISAIAH (OR NARRATOR): He took our sicknesses and carried our diseases.

NARRATOR: One day Jesus and his disciples got into a boat on the **Sea of Galilee**. He said to them:

JESUS: Let's go over to the other side of the lake.

NARRATOR: So, they launched out. As they were sailing, he fell asleep. A windstorm came down on the lake, and they were taking on dangerous amounts of water. The disciples came to him and woke him up.

DISCIPLES: Master, master, we're going to drown!

NARRATOR: Jesus woke up and spoke to the winds and waves.

JESUS: Quiet! Be still!

NARRATOR: Then the wind died down, and the water was completely calm.

JESUS: Why are you so afraid? Where is your faith?

NARRATOR: These disciples were amazed. They said to each other:

DISCIPLES: Who is this? Even the winds and the water obey him!

Power

When Jesus speaks, nature and even death obey him! No problem I face is too big for Jesus to solve.

NARRATOR: Later Jesus returned to **Capernaum**. A large crowd welcomed him because they were all waiting for him. A man named Jairus, a leader of the synagogue, came to him. He fell down at Jesus' feet and begged him:

JAIRUS: Please come to my house. My only daughter, who's about twelve years old, is dying. Please put your hands on her and heal her.

NARRATOR: While Jesus was still talking with the crowd, someone from Jairus' house came up to them with a message.

JAIRUS' SERVANT: Your daughter is dead. Don't bother the teacher anymore.

JESUS: Don't be afraid. Only believe, and she will be healed.

NARRATOR: When Jesus came to Jairus' house, he didn't allow anyone to go inside except Peter, John, James, and the child's parents. Everyone was crying loudly.

JESUS: Don't cry. She isn't dead. She's just sleeping.

NARRATOR: The crowd made fun of him because they knew she was dead. But he again told them to go outside. Then he took the girl by her hand and said:

JESUS: Little girl, get up!

NARRATOR: Her spirit returned, and she got up right away. He told them to give her something to eat. Her parents were amazed, but he ordered them not to tell anyone what had happened.

Review It!

How many miracles did Jesus do when he lived on earth?

Who did Jesus heal?

How did he heal them?

How did Jesus calm a storm on the sea?

Remember It!

SONG: *Jesus in Galilee* (verses 1–2)

Learn these timeline events.

7. John the Baptist put in jail
8. Jesus moves to Capernaum
9. Jesus talks with a woman at a well
10. Jesus heals a nobleman's son
11. Jesus calls his disciples
12. Jesus preaches and heals throughout Galilee

Think About It!

Jesus healed everyone who asked him. What can we learn from that fact?

What does Jesus have power over?

After Jesus calmed the storm, he asked his disciples a question. He also told Jairus the same thing would unlock a miracle for him. What is it? Why do you think it's important in both miracles?

Having Jesus help me isn't something I earn or deserve. It's a free gift from God.

Map It!

Dots show where cities are. Lines show where regions are. Label these places:

- Nazareth
- Bethlehem
- Cana
- Jerusalem
- Jordan River

- Dead Sea
- Capernaum
- Galilee
- Sea of Galilee

© Master the Bible Ministries

Answers in Appendix E Map 1

CHAPTER 3

Who is Jesus?

John 6, Matthew 16

DIRECTIONS: Read the story to yourself. Or read it as a family with each person reading a different part aloud. When you come to a place name in **bold**, draw a fish in that location on a map in Appendix E.

Feeds 5,000 and Walks on Water | John 6

NARRATOR: One day Jesus went to the other side of the **Sea of Galilee** (near **Bethsaida**). A large crowd followed him because they saw how he healed people who were sick. Seeing this large crowd coming toward him, Jesus said to Philip, one of his disciples:

JESUS: Where can we go to buy bread for these people to eat?

NARRATOR: He asked Philip this question to test him. Jesus already knew what he was going to do.

Followers

I can follow Jesus because he meets a need I have. I can follow him because that's what everyone else is doing. But following him for those reasons won't change my life. If I follow him because I realize who he is—worthy of everything I am—then I'm changed.

PHILIP: If I had eight months' pay, it wouldn't be enough to give them all a little bite!

NARRATOR: Another disciple named Andrew, Peter's brother, said:

ANDREW: There's a boy here who has five loaves of bread and two small fish. But what good are these with so many people?

JESUS: Have the people sit down.

NARRATOR: So, everyone sat down. There were about five thousand men plus women and children. Jesus took the bread and thanked God for it. Then he handed it to his disciples to give to the people. He did the same thing with the fish. People ate as much as they wanted. When they were full, Jesus said to his disciples:

JESUS: Gather up the broken pieces that are left over. We don't want anything to be lost.

NARRATOR: So, they gathered them up and filled twelve baskets with the leftovers. When the people saw this sign that Jesus did, they said:

CROWDS: This has got to be the prophet we have been expecting to come into the world.

NARRATOR: Jesus realized they were about to come and force him to be king of Israel. So, he went away to the mountain by himself. Meanwhile, his disciples went down to the sea. They got into their boat and were going over to **Capernaum**. It was dark now, and Jesus hadn't joined them. A strong wind began to toss the sea. When they had rowed three or four miles (five or six kilometers), they saw Jesus walking on the sea. He was getting closer to the boat. They saw him and were scared. But he said to them:

JESUS: It is I. Don't be afraid.

NARRATOR: So, they agreed to take him into the boat. Right away the boat was at the place where they were going.

Real Mission

Jesus didn't come to heal or teach or be a wonderful example. His real mission was to die and rise again. What is the real mission of your life? God has written down a plan for everyone's life. When we follow it, we find rewards and excitement and blessings—just like Jesus did.

Peter Realizes Who Jesus Is

Matthew 16

NARRATOR: When Jesus traveled to the area near **Caesarea-Philippi**, he asked his disciples:

JESUS: Who do people say that I, the Son of Man, am?

DISCIPLE 1: Some say John the Baptizer. Some say Elijah.

DISCIPLE 2: Others say Jeremiah or one of the prophets.

JESUS: But who do *you* say that I am?

PETER: You are the Christ, the Son of the living God.

JESUS: Blessed are you, Simon, son of Jonah! For people didn't help you realize this. My Father in heaven showed this to you. I declare that you are Peter. On this rock I will build my church, and the gates of hell will not be able to destroy it. I will give to you the keys of the Kingdom of Heaven. Whatever you lock on earth will be locked in heaven. And whatever you unlock on earth will be unlocked in heaven.

NARRATOR: Then he commanded the disciples not to tell anyone that he was the Christ (God's Anointed). Starting then, Jesus began to tell his disciples:

JESUS: We must go to Jerusalem. There I'll be handed over to the chief priests and teachers of the law who will sentence me to death. They'll hand me over to people who aren't Jews, who will make fun of me and kill me. But three days later, I'll rise from the dead!

Review It!

How many loaves of bread and fish did the boy offer Jesus? Was it enough to feed the crowd?

How did Jesus feed the crowd?

What did Jesus do after he fed the crowd?

Who did Peter say Jesus is?

Remember It!

SONG: *Jesus in Galilee* (verses 3–4)

Learn these timeline events.

13. Jesus heals a leper, disabled man, crippled, withered hand and more
14. Jesus picks 12 apostles
15. Many women Jesus healed follow him
16. Preaches a sermon on a mountain
17. Heals a soldier's servant
18. Raises a widow's son from the dead

Why did Jesus feed the crowd?

How did the crowd react to this miracle? Do you think they changed?

Why do you think Jesus asked his disciples who they thought he was rather than telling them the answer?

God has written down a mission for my life just like he did for Jesus.

Map It!

Dots show where cities are. Lines show where regions are. Label these places:

- Nazareth
- Bethlehem
- Cana
- Jerusalem
- Jordan River
- Dead Sea

- Capernaum
- Galilee
- Sea of Galilee
- Bethsaida
- Caesarea-Philippi

Answers in Appendix E Map 1

CHAPTER 4

Jesus Follows God's Plan

John 12; Luke 22, Matt. 26

DIRECTIONS: Read the story to yourself. Or read it as a family with each person reading a different part aloud. When you come to a place name in **bold**, draw a palm branch in that location on a map in Appendix E.

Jesus Enters Jerusalem like a King
John 12, Luke 22

NARRATOR: A huge crowd had come to **Jerusalem** to celebrate the holiday called Passover. When they heard that Jesus was coming to Jerusalem, they took branches from palm trees and went out to meet him. They cried out:

CROWD 1: Hosanna! Blessed is he who comes in the name of the Lord!

CROWD 2: Blessed is the King of Israel!

Praise

Jesus deserved the praise people gave him when he entered Jerusalem. When we praise Jesus, it lines up our minds and spirits with God. It helps us to see and hear what God wants to show us.

NARRATOR: Jesus found a young donkey and rode into Jerusalem sitting on it. He did this to fulfill what the prophet told long before:

Those who live in Jerusalem, don't be afraid. Look! Your King is coming, sitting on a young donkey.

His disciples didn't understand at first that Jesus was fulfilling this prophecy. But later, after Jesus rose from death, they remembered that this prophecy was written about him. And they remembered that the people had done these things to him.

Judas Decides to Betray Jesus

Luke 22:1-6

NARRATOR: While the crowd was welcoming Jesus into Jerusalem like a king, the chief priests and teachers of the law were thinking about how they could have him killed. But they were afraid to arrest Jesus when the crowds were around. Then Satan entered into Judas, one of Jesus' twelve apostles. He went to the chief priests and said:

JUDAS: What will you give me if I hand Jesus over to you?

PRIEST: Thirty pieces of silver.

JUDAS: I will watch for the right time to hand Jesus over to you, when there is no crowd around.

NARRATOR: The chief priests were delighted. They counted out thirty pieces of silver and gave them to Judas.

Last Passover

Luke 22:14-20; Matthew 26:36-50

NARRATOR: When it was time to eat the Passover meal, Jesus sat down with his apostles. He said:

JESUS: I have really looked forward to eating this Passover meal with you before I suffer. I tell you; I certainly won't eat the Passover meal again until it's celebrated in God's Kingdom.

NARRATOR: He took one of the cups that are part of the Passover meal. After he gave thanks, he said:

JESUS: Take this and pass it around. I tell you; I won't drink wine again until God's Kingdom comes.

NARRATOR: He took bread that is part of the Passover meal. He broke it and gave it to them, saying:

JESUS: This is my body, which is given for you. Do this in memory of me.

NARRATOR: He took the cup that comes after the meal is eaten and said:

Special Time

Jesus looked forward to spending time with his disciples. He also looks forward to spending time with you. Each moment you spend with Jesus fills his heart with so much joy.

JESUS: This cup is the new agreement made with my blood, which is poured out for you.

Jesus is Arrested

Matthew 26

NARRATOR: After they finished celebrating the Passover meal, Jesus took his disciples to a garden called Gethsemane, where he liked to pray.

JESUS: Sit here, while I go over there and pray.

NARRATOR: He took with him Peter, James, and John. He became extremely sad and troubled.

JESUS: My soul is overwhelmed with sadness. I'm feeling close to death. Stay here and keep watch with me.

NARRATOR: Jesus went a little farther, fell down on his face, and prayed:

JESUS: My Father, if it's possible, let this cup of suffering pass away from me. But don't do what I want. Do what you want.

NARRATOR: After he prayed this, Jesus came to his disciples and found them sleeping. He said to Peter:

JESUS: Couldn't you keep watch with me for one hour? Watch and pray so you won't sin when you're tempted to. Your spirit is willing to do what's right, but your body is weak.

NARRATOR: While he was still talking, Judas came with a large crowd from the chief priest and elders. They were carrying swords and clubs. Now Judas had given them a sign:

JUDAS: The one I kiss is the one. Arrest him.

NARRATOR: Immediately he came to Jesus, kissed him, and said:

JUDAS: Hello, Rabbi!

JESUS: Friend, why are you here?

NARRATOR: Then they grabbed Jesus and arrested him.

Review It!

What animal did Jesus ride on when he entered Jerusalem for Passover?
What did people put on the ground in front of him?

How did the crowd welcome Jesus to Jerusalem?

What did Judas decide to do?

Who did Jesus eat and pray with? Who arrested him?

Remember It!

SONG: *Jesus in Galilee* (verses 4-5)

Learn these timeline events.

19. Calms a storm
20. Casts out demons in Gadarenes
21. Heals a woman with a blood problem
22. Raises' Jairus' girl from the dead
23. Nazareth rejects him
24. Sends disciples out to preach and heal

Why do you think Jesus really looked forward to spending time with his disciples?

What new meaning did Jesus give to the bread and wine at Passover?

Judas did what he wanted to do, while Jesus did what God wanted him to do. Which path led to the better ending? Why do you think doing what God wants makes us better off than doing what we want to do?

Jesus looks forward to spending time with me.

Map It!

Dots show where cities are. Lines show where regions are. Label these places:

- Nazareth
- Bethlehem
- Cana
- Jerusalem
- Jordan River
- Dead Sea
- Capernaum

- Galilee
- Sea of Galilee
- Bethsaida
- Caesarea-Philippi
- Judea
- Samaria
- Bethany

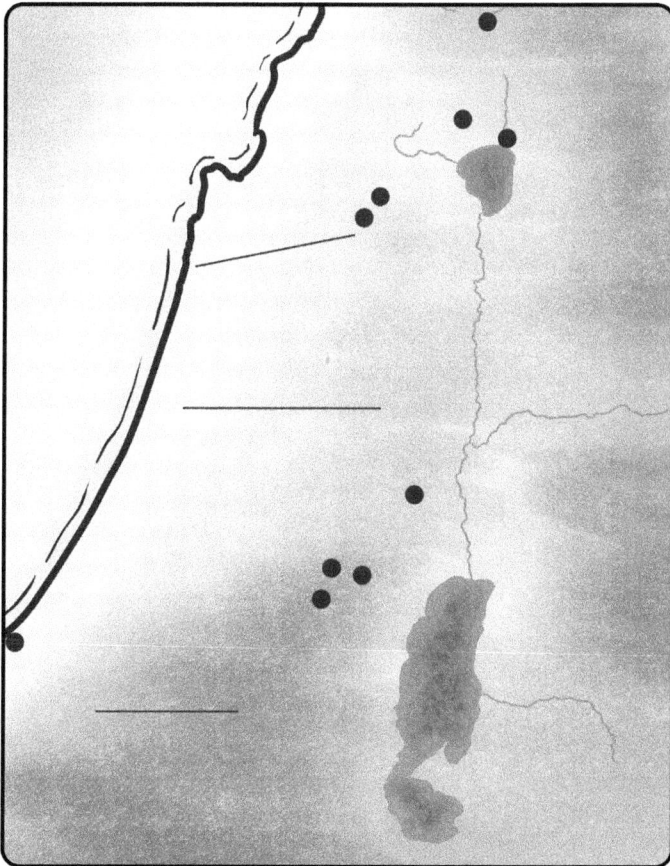

Answers in Appendix E Map 1

CHAPTER 5

Jesus Dies and Rises!

Luke 23, Matthew 28

DIRECTIONS: Read the story to yourself. Or read it as a family with each person reading a different part aloud. When you come to a place name in **bold**, draw a cross in that location on a map in Appendix E.

Jesus Dies

Luke 23

NARRATOR: The governor Pilate called together the chief priests, the rulers, and the people. He said to them:

PILATE: You brought this man to me, claiming he's turning the people against the government. Look, I've examined him in front of you and I've found no basis for the things you're accusing him of.

NARRATOR: But they shouted:

CROWD: Crucify! Crucify him!

PILATE: Why? What evil has this man done? I haven't found a reason to have him put to death. So, I'll have him whipped and let him go.

NARRATOR: But the crowd shouted loudly that Jesus should be crucified. The shouts of the crowd and the chief priests won. Pilate ordered that Jesus be crucified just as they wanted. Jesus was led along with two criminals to a place called The Skull. There they crucified him with the criminals, one on his right and one on his left.

JESUS: Father, forgive them. They don't know what they're doing.

NARRATOR: About noon darkness came over the whole land until three o'clock in the afternoon. The sun's light failed. The veil in the temple, which kept people out of God's presence, was torn in two from top to bottom. In a loud voice Jesus cried:

JESUS: Father, into your hands I commit my spirit!

NARRATOR: Right after he said this, Jesus took his last breath. When the Roman commander saw what had happened, he said:

SOLDIER: Certainly this was a righteous man.

NARRATOR: When the large crowds saw this, they went home beating their chests to show how sad they were. The people who knew Jesus, including the women who had followed him from Galilee, stood at a distance. They were watching these things. A man named Joseph asked Pilate:

JOSEPH: Could I have Jesus' body, so I can bury it?

NARRATOR: So, Joseph took Jesus' body, wrapped it in a cloth, and laid it in a new tomb that was cut into stone. Two of Jesus' followers, Mary Magdalene and another woman named Mary, were sitting across from the tomb. They saw where Jesus was buried.

Forgiveness

Jesus' death took God's punishment for my sin. Anything I've done is totally and forever forgiven when I ask Jesus to forgive me. The record of my sin is erased, and heaven doesn't remember it anymore.

Jesus Rises from Death
Matthew 28

NARRATOR: Very early on the first day of the week, Mary Magdalene and the other Mary came to see the tomb. There was a great earthquake because an angel had come down and rolled the stone away from the door of the tomb. He was sitting on the stone. He looked like lightening, and his clothes were as white as snow (or rice or puffy clouds). The guards were so afraid of him that they shook and fell down like dead men.

ANGEL: Don't be afraid. I know you're looking for Jesus. He was crucified. He's not here. He's risen, just like he said. Come and see the place where the Lord was lying. Go quickly and tell his disciples, "He has risen from the dead. He's going ahead of you to **Galilee**. There you'll see him." Look, I've told you.

Victory

What does Jesus' victory over death mean for me? When I trust in Jesus, he shares with me everything he won. Then he makes me like him. Anything Jesus did, I can do! Even death will not win. I will live with Jesus forever in heaven!

NARRATOR: Quickly, they left the tomb, full of fear and joy. They ran to tell the disciples what the angel said. As they were going, Jesus met them:

JESUS: Hello!

NARRATOR: They grabbed hold of his feet and worshiped him.

JESUS: Don't be afraid. Go tell my brothers that they should go into Galilee. They'll see me there.

NARRATOR: While they were going, some of the guards went into the city (of **Jerusalem**). They told the chief priests everything that had happened. After gathering the elders and making a plan, the priests gave a large sum of money to the soldiers.

PRIEST: Tell people, "His disciples came at night and stole his body while we were sleeping." If this story is reported to the governor, we will win him over and keep you out of trouble.

NARRATOR: So, the soldiers took the money and did as they were told. Their story has been told among the Jews even until today.

So, the eleven disciples went to Galilee, to the mountain where Jesus had told them to go. When they saw him, they worshiped him. But some doubted.

JESUS: All authority in heaven and earth has been given to me. Go, and make all nations disciples. Baptize them in the name of the Father and of the Son and of the Holy Spirit. Teach them to do everything I commanded you. See, I'm with you always, even to the very end. Amen.

Review It!

Who wanted Jesus to die? Who did not want him to die?

What did Jesus say when he was on the cross?

Who saw Jesus die? Who saw his body placed in a tomb?

Who saw Jesus risen from death?

Remember It!

SONG: *Jesus in Galilee* (verses 5-6)

Learn these timeline events.

25. Feeds 5,000
26. Walks on water
27. Heals a girl from Tyre area
28. Feeds 4,000
29. Peter says Jesus is God's Son
30. Jesus shines in glory

Think About It!

Why did Jesus die?

What evidence does the Bible give that Jesus really did die and rise from death?

What did Jesus gain through his suffering?

Jesus forgives my sin and erases every record of it.

Dots show where cities are. Lines show where regions are. Label these places:

- Nazareth
- Bethlehem
- Cana
- Jerusalem
- Jordan River
- Dead Sea
- Capernaum

- Galilee
- Sea of Galilee
- Bethsaida
- Caesarea-Philippi
- Judea
- Samaria
- Bethany

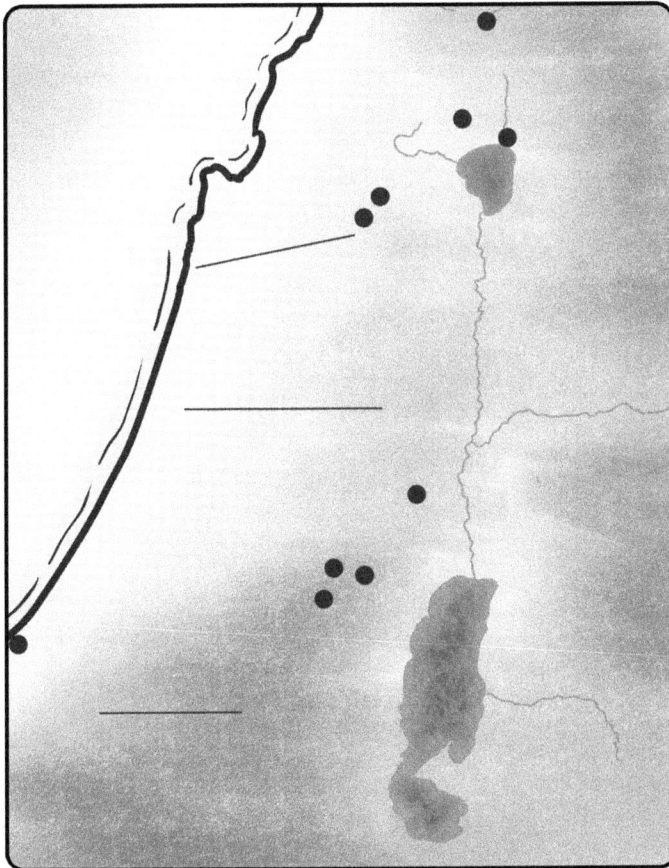

Answers in Appendix E Map 1

CHAPTER 6

The Church Begins

Acts 1-2

DIRECTIONS: Read the story to yourself. Or read it as a family with each person reading a different part aloud. When you come to a place name in **bold**, draw fire in that location on a map in Appendix E.

Jesus Goes Back to Heaven
Acts 1

LUKE (THE NARRATOR): I wrote earlier about all the things Jesus did. I told about what he taught from the beginning until the day he was taken up to heaven. Before he left, he gave orders through the Holy Spirit to the apostles he had chosen. He appeared to them for forty days, giving them clear signs and proof that he was alive. And he continued teaching them about the kingdom of God.
Once when they were all together, he told them:

JESUS: Don't leave **Jerusalem**. Stay there and wait for the gift the Father promised that I've told you about. John baptized with water. But a few days from now, you will be baptized with the Holy Spirit.

APOSTLES: Lord, are you going to give the kingdom back to Israel at this time?

JESUS: You're not meant to know the times or dates the Father has kept under his control. But you will receive power when the Holy Spirit comes on you. And you will tell everyone what you saw me do—people in Jerusalem, in **Judea** and **Samaria**, and everywhere on earth.

LUKE (THE NARRATOR): After Jesus said this, he was taken up into heaven. As the disciples watched, he was lifted up until a cloud hid him from their view. While they were staring up into the sky, two men in white clothes came to them.

MEN IN WHITE CLOTHES: Men from **Galilee**, why are you standing there looking up at the sky? Jesus was taken from you to heaven. He'll come again the same way you saw him go into heaven.

Holy Spirit Comes

Acts 2

LUKE (THE NARRATOR): On the holiday Pentecost, Jesus' followers were all together in one place. Suddenly, a sound like a violent wind came from heaven and filled the house where they were sitting. They saw tongues that looked like flames of fire resting on every one of them. And they were all filled with the Holy Spirit. They began talking in different languages as the Spirit gave them the power to do.

Now godly Jews from every part of the world were staying in **Jerusalem** to celebrate Pentecost. When they heard the sound, a crowd gathered because they each heard the believers speaking in their own language. Surprised, they said:

CROWD 1: Aren't all these people from **Galilee**?

CROWD 2: Why do we each hear them speaking in the languages of the countries where we were born?

CROWD 3: We hear languages from all over the world—different parts of the Middle East, Africa, and Europe!

CROWD 4: They're all talking about the wonderful things God has done!

LUKE (THE NARRATOR): They were all amazed and confused. They were saying:

CROWD 1: What does this mean?

LUKE (THE NARRATOR): But others were making fun of them:

God on the Inside

When Jesus walked the earth, you had to travel to him to get a miracle or a teaching or a hug. Then God's Holy Spirit came. God moved from living on the outside to living inside his people. We can talk to God and be with him all the time.

CROWD 5: They've had too much new wine!

LUKE (THE NARRATOR): But Peter stood up with the other eleven apostles:

PETER: People of Jerusalem, I'll explain this to you. These people aren't drunk. It's only 9 o'clock in the morning. What's happening is what the prophet Joel predicted. He said that in the last days God will send his Spirit on everyone. He said: "Your sons and your daughters will hear God's words and speak them. Your young men will see visions. And your old men will have dreams from God. And on my servants, both men and women, I will send my Spirit. And they will hear my words and speak them. And anyone who calls on the name of the Lord will be saved."

People of Israel, listen to this! Jesus of **Nazareth** was a man who had God's approval. You saw the signs and miracles he did that made God's approval of him clear. God decided long ago that Jesus would be handed over to you. Along with evil people, you put him to death by nailing him to a cross.

Holy Spirit

God gives me his Spirit so I will become fully like him. Holy Spirit gives me God's love, power, and direction. He gives me the ability to listen to God. And he gives me power to live God's plan for my life.

But God raised him from death. It was impossible for death to hold him in its power. We all saw ourselves that God raised Jesus back to life. So let all Israel know for sure that God has made Jesus both Lord and Christ—the same Jesus that you nailed to a cross.

LUKE (THE NARRATOR): When the people heard this, they were troubled. They said to Peter and the other Apostles:

CROWD 1: What should we do?

PETER: Change what you're doing and thinking. Then be baptized in the name of Jesus Christ for the forgiveness of your sins. Then the Holy Spirit will be given to you, too. For the promise is for you and for your children and for everyone who is far away—everyone that the Lord our God chooses.

LUKE (THE NARRATOR): Peter told them many other things, begging them:

PETER: Save yourself from these evil people.

LUKE (THE NARRATOR): About 3,000 people accepted his message and were baptized that day.

Review It!

Who saw Jesus return to heaven?

Who was filled with Holy Spirit on Pentecost?

How many people were baptized after Peter preached?

From where were the people who heard the apostles speaking in different languages?

Remember It!

SONG: *Jesus in Galilee* (verses 6-7) **and** *Jesus in Judea* (verse 1)

Learn these timeline events.

31. Jesus casts a demon from a boy
32. Jesus heals a man born blind
33. Jesus sends out 72 disciples
34. Jesus teaches at Mary and Martha's house
35. Jesus says he is One with God

Think About It!

Why was it important for Jesus' disciples to receive God's Holy Spirit? What did Jesus say Holy Spirit would give them?

Why do you think God's Holy Spirit looked like tongues of fire? What does that picture tell us about Holy Spirit? What do we use tongues for? What is fire like?

How did the disciples change after they were filled with God's Holy Spirit? What did Peter preach?

God wants people from every nation and culture in his family.

Dots show where cities are. Lines show where regions are. Label this place:

- Damascus

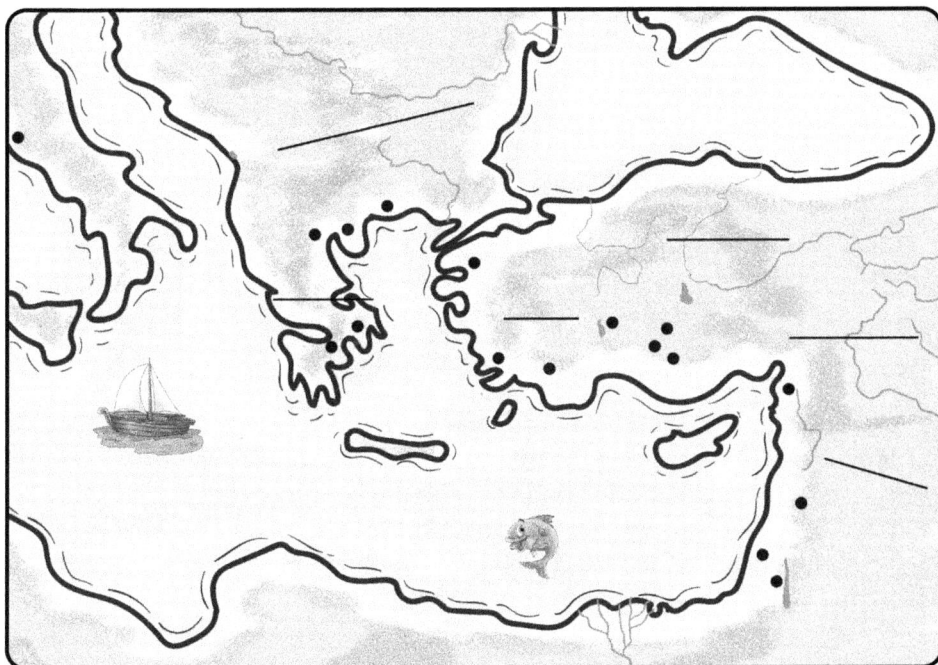

Answers in Appendix E Map 2

CHAPTER 7

Jesus' Followers Heal and Love

Acts 3-4

DIRECTIONS: Read the story to yourself. Or read it as a family with each person reading a different part aloud. When you come to a place name in **bold**, draw a heart in that location on a map in Appendix E.

Peter and John Heal
Acts 3-4

LUKE (THE NARRATOR): Peter and John were going to the temple (in **Jerusalem**) at 3 o'clock in the afternoon, the time for prayer. They passed a man who hadn't been able to use his legs ever since he was born. Every day, people would carry him close to the temple so that he could beg. Seeing Peter and John going to the temple, he asked them for money.

PETER AND JOHN: Look at us!

LUKE (THE NARRATOR): Hoping they would give him something, the man looked at them closely.

I Can, Too

People who believe in Jesus can do the things Jesus did. We can pray for people's healing and speak boldly about Jesus. We can give generously and love other people deeply.

PETER: I don't have silver or gold. But what I do have, I give to you. In the name of Jesus Christ of **Nazareth**, stand up on your feet and walk.

LUKE (THE NARRATOR): Taking the man by his right hand, Peter lifted him up. Right away, his feet and ankles became strong. Jumping up, he walked into the temple with them, walking and jumping and praising God.

MAN: Praise God!

LUKE (THE NARRATOR): All the people saw him walking and praising God. They recognized him as the man who would beg for money near the temple. They were amazed and surprised at what had happened.

PETER: People of Israel, why are you so surprised? Why are you looking at us like it was our great power or virtue that healed this man? The name of Jesus Christ of Nazareth made this man completely well. There is no other name that will save us.

LUKE (THE NARRATOR): Many people who heard Peter's message believed. Now the number of men who believed in Jesus was about 5,000.

Believers Love Powerfully

Acts 4

LUKE (THE NARRATOR): All the believers prayed together:

DISCIPLES: Lord, give your servants power to speak your word without fear. And while we're speaking boldly, stretch out your hand to heal and to do miraculous signs and wonders through the name of your holy servant Jesus.

LUKE (THE NARRATOR): When they stopped praying, the place where they were shook violently. They were all filled with the Holy Spirit and preached the word of God boldly.

And they all agreed in their hearts and minds. No one claimed that something they owned was their own but instead shared everything so that none of them was in need. Everyone who owned land or houses would sell them, bring money, and put it at the feet of the apostles for them to give to anyone who was in need.

Love

The disciples loved each other so much that they didn't consider anything they owned as their own. They are a picture of how much God loves us. God doesn't consider anything he owns as his own. He gladly gives us anything he has because he loves us so much.

Review It!

How did Peter and John heal a man who couldn't walk?

What did the man do after he was healed?

How many followers did Jesus have after Peter and John healed the man?

What did the believers do if they heard someone had a need?

Remember It!

SONG: *Jesus in Judea* (verse 2)

Learn these timeline events.

36. Jesus heals dropsy on the Sabbath
37. Jesus raises Lazarus from the dead
38. Jesus heals 10 lepers
39. Jesus blesses children
40. Jesus teaches a rich young ruler

Why did Peter and John heal the man who couldn't use his legs?

If you had been one of the people who saw the man jumping and walking, what would you have thought?

Why did the believers pray that God would do miracles and signs as they told people about Jesus? How did God respond to their prayer? Do you think he was happy they prayed that?

Jesus picked me to do what he did.

Map It!

Dots show where cities are. Lines show where regions are. Label these places:

- Damascus
- Antioch
- Cyprus

Answers in Appendix E Map 2

CHAPTER 8

Samaritans and Africans Believe

Acts 8

DIRECTIONS: Read the story to yourself. Or read it as a family with each person reading a different part aloud. When you come to a place name in **bold**, draw a smiley face in that location on a map in Appendix E.

Samaritans Believe
Acts 8

LUKE (THE NARRATOR): At that time, the church in **Jerusalem** began to be attacked and treated badly. Everyone but the Apostles left Jerusalem, moving to **Judea** and **Samaria**. Everywhere they went, they told people about Jesus.

PHILIP: I'll go to Samaria to tell the people there about Jesus.

Miracles

Who can do miracles? Even though Philip wasn't an apostle, he prayed in Jesus' name and miracles happened. Jesus loves it when we pray for people in his name and expect a miracle.

LUKE (THE NARRATOR): When the Samarian people saw the signs that Philip did, they paid attention to what he was teaching. With a scream, evil spirits came out of people. And a lot of people who were sick and who couldn't walk were healed.

CROWD: This is wonderful! Look at what God is doing!

LUKE (THE NARRATOR): There was a man there named Simon who had practiced magic. Claiming he was someone great, he had amazed all the people of Samaria. Everyone, from the least important to the most important, said:

CROWD: This man is the power of the great God.

LUKE (THE NARRATOR): They paid attention to him because for a long time he had held them under his power. But a lot of them believed in the good news Philip told them about the kingdom of God and Jesus. They were baptized, both men and women. Simon himself was baptized. Following Philip around, he was amazed at the signs and wonders he saw.

When the Apostles in Jerusalem heard that Samaritans had believed, they sent Peter and John. When they arrived, they prayed for them so they would receive the Holy Spirit. Up to that time, Holy Spirit had not come on any of them. They had just been baptized in Jesus' name. Then they put their hands on them, and the Holy Spirit came on them. Now when Simon saw that the Holy Spirit was given by the Apostles laying hands on people, he offered them money, saying:

SIMON: Give me this power, so that when I put my hands on people, they may receive the Holy Spirit.

PETER: May your money be destroyed with you! Do you think the gift of God can be purchased with money? You have no part or share in what we're doing because your heart is not right before God. Change what you're doing and thinking. Ask God to forgive you for your evil thoughts. I see that you're chained by bitterness and sin.

SIMON: Pray for me to the Lord so these things you just said won't happen to me.

LUKE (THE NARRATOR): The Apostles returned to Jerusalem.

Angels

Why did an angel talk to Philip? Angels are spirits that God created to serve him (Hebrews 1:7). They also serve God's people (Hebrews 1:14). Angels often bring messages from God.

Africans Believe

Acts 8

LUKE (THE NARRATOR): Then an angel said to Philip:

ANGEL: Get up and head south. Go to the road that goes from **Jerusalem** to **Gaza** through the wilderness.

LUKE (THE NARRATOR): When Philip went there, he saw a man from Ethiopia. He was a servant of Queen Candace and carried great authority. He was in charge of the royal treasury. He had come to Jerusalem to worship and was returning home. Sitting in his chariot, he was reading the book of Isaiah. The Spirit said to Philip:

HOLY SPIRIT: Go over and join his chariot.

LUKE (THE NARRATOR): Running up to him, Philip noticed he was reading Isaiah. He asked:

PHILIP: Do you understand what you are reading?

ETHIOPIAN: How can I when I don't have anyone to explain it to me?

LUKE (THE NARRATOR): He invited Philip to come sit with him.

ETHIOPIAN: Who is the prophet speaking about? Himself or someone else?

LUKE (THE NARRATOR): Starting with the words he was reading, Philip explained the good news of Jesus. As they traveled on, they came to some water. The Ethiopian said:

ETHIOPIAN: Look, here's some water! Can you baptize me right now?

LUKE (THE NARRATOR): So, the two of them went into the water, and Philip baptized him. And when they came up out of the water, the Spirit took Philip away. The Ethiopian continued his journey full of joy. Philip found himself at a town in **Samaria.** He went through all the towns in Samaria preaching until he came to **Caesarea**.

Review It!

Why did Jesus' followers leave Jerusalem?

Why did the people in Samaria listen to Philip's message?

How did Philip share about Jesus to the Ethiopian? How did he know where to meet him?

Where did Philip share the good news? Where did he meet the Ethiopian?

Remember It!

SONG: *Jesus in Judea* (verse 3)

Learn these timeline events.

41. Jesus explains he will die and rise again
42. James and John ask for positions of power
43. Jesus heals blind Bartimaeus
44. Jesus eats with Zacchaeus
45. Jesus is crucified
46. Jesus' body is placed in a tomb
47. Jesus rises from the dead

Think About It!

What sorts of miracles did Philip do in Samaria? Do you think people would have listened to his message if he had not done miracles? Why or why not?

Simon the magician thought he could buy Holy Spirit's power with money. How do we receive the power of God's Spirit? Why is that better than buying it?

Why do you think God wanted Philip to tell the Ethiopian official about Jesus?

God loves it when I tell other people about Jesus.

Map It!

Dots show where cities are. Lines show where regions are. Label these places:

- Damascus
- Antioch
- Cyprus
- Antioch in Pisidia
- Iconium

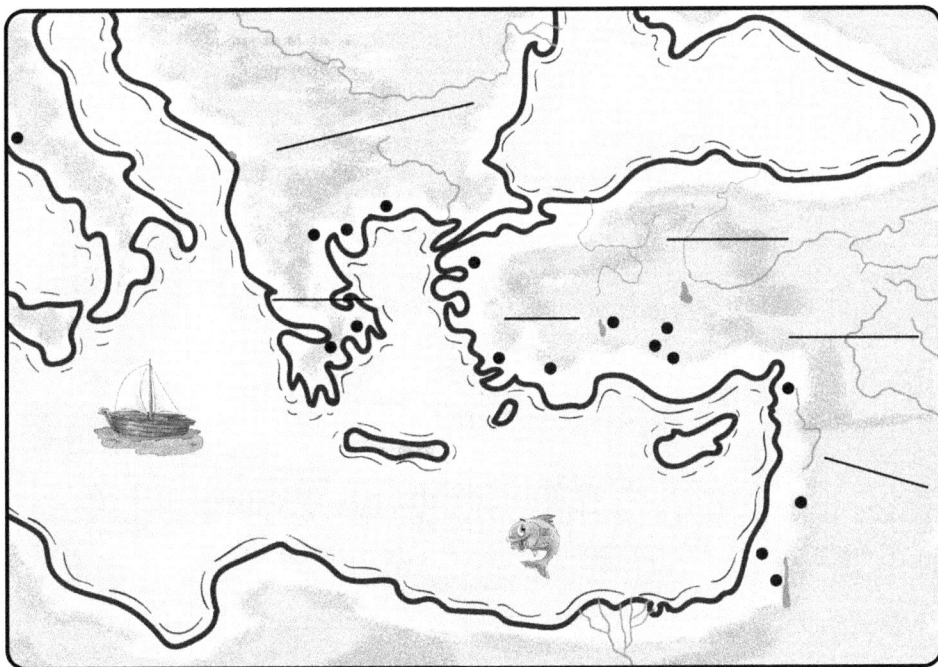

Answers in Appendix E Map 2

CHAPTER 9

Paul's First Journey

Acts 13-14

DIRECTIONS: Read the story to yourself. Or read it as a family with each person reading a different part aloud. When you come to a place name in **bold**, draw a number 1 in that location on a map in Appendix E.

First Journey Begins

Acts 13

LUKE (THE NARRATOR): In the church at **Antioch**, there were prophets and teachers from different parts of the world. While they were worshiping and fasting, the Holy Spirit spoke:

HOLY SPIRIT: Set apart Barnabas and Saul for the special work I've called them to do.

LUKE (THE NARRATOR): After praying and fasting, they laid their hands on them and sent them off. They sailed to **Cyprus**. There they preached God's word in the Jewish synagogues. When they had traveled through the whole island, they met in the capital a Jewish magician called Elymas. This false prophet was with the governor Sergius Paulus. Now the governor asked for Barnabas and Saul so that they could explain their message to him. But the magician Elymas opposed them, trying to turn the governor away from their message. But Saul, also called Paul—filled with the Holy Spirit—said to Elymas:

PAUL: You are full of false tricks and evil ways! You're a son of the evil one and you hate everything good. How long will you turn people from the right ways of the Lord? Now God's hand is on you, and you will be blind for a time!

LUKE (THE NARRATOR): Right away, a dark mist came on him, and he went around looking for someone to guide him by the hand. When the governor saw what happened, he believed. He was amazed at the teaching of the Lord.

Then Paul and Barnabas left Cyprus and traveled to **Antioch in Pisidia**. On the Sabbath (Saturday), they went into the synagogue. The leaders asked:

SYNAGOGUE LEADER: Brothers, do you have something encouraging to say to these people? If you do, please tell us.

PAUL: Men of Israel, God gave our ancestors a king named David. From the family line of David, God brought a Savior, Jesus, just as he promised. But the people who live in **Jerusalem** didn't recognize him. Although they found no reason to put him to death, they asked for him to be killed. Then they took him down from the cross and placed him in a tomb. But God raised him from the dead, and he appeared to his disciples for many days. I want you to know that through Jesus your sins can be forgiven.

LUKE (THE NARRATOR): As Paul and Barnabas were leaving, the people told them:

CROWD: We'd really like to hear you speak about these things next week.

LUKE (THE NARRATOR): The next week, almost the entire city came to hear the word of the Lord. But when the Jews saw the crowds, they became jealous. They started to speak against what Paul was saying.

You're Special

God has a special plan for your life just like he had a special plan for Paul and Barnabas. God doesn't care if you're not fully mature. He just wants you to be willing to start the journey with him.

BARNABAS: Since you don't consider yourselves good enough for eternal life, we're turning to the people who aren't Jews. God has said, "I've made you a light to the nations to bring salvation to the entire earth."

CROWD: Yeah! Praise God!

LUKE (THE NARRATOR): The word of the Lord was spreading through the entire region. But the Jews stirred up important women and men in the city. Together, they threw Paul and Barnabas out of their region.

LUKE (THE NARRATOR): Paul and Barnabas traveled to **Iconium**, where the same thing happened. When they spoke in the Jewish synagogue, a large number of Jews and non-Jews believed. But the ones who didn't believe stirred up trouble. Paul and Barnabas stayed in Iconium for a long time. Speaking with boldness for the Lord, they performed miracles and wonders that confirmed what they were saying. But the city was divided.

CROWD 1: We like Paul and Barnabas!

CROWD 2: We don't like Paul and Barnabas!

LUKE (THE NARRATOR): When some Jews and non-Jews tried to kill them, Paul and Barnabas fled to **Lystra**. In Lystra, Paul noticed a man who from birth couldn't use his feet. The man was listening carefully to Paul. When Paul saw that he had faith to be healed, he said in a loud voice:

Courage

Like Paul, not everyone will be excited that we decided to live for God. But God will give us friends to help us.

PAUL: Stand up on your feet!

LUKE (THE NARRATOR): So, the man leaped up and began to walk. When the crowds saw what Paul had done, they shouted:

CROWD: The gods have come down to us looking like humans!

LUKE (THE NARRATOR): The priest of the temple of Zeus came out with bulls. Everyone wanted to sacrifice to Paul and Barnabas. But Paul rushed into the crowd shouting:

PAUL: Why are you doing this? We're men just like you. We're telling you about how you should turn from idols who can't do anything to worship the living God. He's the one who made heaven and earth and everything in them. He's the one who gives you rain and food. And he's the one who makes your hearts happy.

LUKE (THE NARRATOR): When Paul said this, he barely stopped them from sacrificing to him. But then Jews from **Antioch [in Pisidia]** and Iconium arrived. They won the crowds over. So, they stoned Paul and dragged him outside the city when they thought he was dead. But when the disciples surrounded him, he got up.

Paul and Barnabas went to **Derbe** to preach. Then they decided to return to Lystra, Iconium, and Antioch in Pisidia. They encouraged the believers and chose leaders for them. Then they returned to where they started.

Review It!

What did God tell Paul and Barnabas about their job before they started out?

Where did Paul and Barnabas go first? Who believed their message? Who was against them?

Where else did Paul and Barnabas go? Who was for them and who was against them?

Whom did Paul heal in Lystra?

Remember It!

SONG: *What Happened when Jesus went back to Heaven?*

Learn these timeline events.

48. Jesus Returns to Heaven
49. Holy Spirit comes at Pentecost
50. Peter and John heal a disabled man
51. Believers share everything in common and are persecuted
52. Philip preaches in Samaria

Think About It!

Put the message Paul shared in your own words. (Hint: Look at what Paul preached in Antioch in Pisidia.) Why do you think some people opposed this message? Why did some people believe it?

Why did people in Lystra think Paul and Barnabas were gods? What does that tell us about the gods they worshiped?

How did the message about Jesus spread? What does the way it spread tell us about God?

God has a special plan for my life.

Map It!

Dots show where cities are.
Lines show where regions are.
Label these places:

- Damascus
- Antioch
- Cyprus
- Antioch in Pisidia
- Iconium
- Lystra
- Derbe

Draw a line connecting the places Paul visited on his first journey:

- Antioch
- Cyprus
- Antioch in Pisidia
- Iconium
- Lystra
- Derbe

Answers in Appendix E Map 2

© Master the Bible Ministries

CHAPTER 10

Paul's Second Journey

Acts 15-18

DIRECTIONS: Read the story to yourself. Or read it as a family with each person reading a different part aloud. When you come to a place name in **bold**, draw a number 2 in that location on a map in Appendix E.

Paul's Second Journey Begins   Acts 15-16

PAUL: Barnabas, let's go back and visit the believers in all the towns where we preached the word of God.

LUKE (THE NARRATOR): Disagreeing about who should go with them, Paul and Barnabas formed two teams. Barnabas took Mark and sailed to **Cyprus**. Paul chose Silas. They traveled through **Syria** and **Cilicia**, strengthening the churches.

After Paul and Cyrus had done everything, they planned to do, they didn't return to Antioch. They felt there was somewhere else they were supposed to share about Jesus. But they weren't sure where God wanted them to go. Many times, they tried to travel to a new region, but God stopped them. Wandering awhile, they arrived at Troas. There Paul had a vision at night where a man begged:

MAN: Come to **Macedonia** and help us!

LUKE (THE NARRATOR): Immediately, we left for Macedonia. At **Philippi**, we met

Lydia

Lydia was a successful merchant who sold purple cloth. She was the first person to believe in Jesus in Macedonia—and Western Europe!

a woman named Lydia. The Lord opened her heart, and she believed Paul's message. She urged:

LYDIA: If you consider me a believer in the Lord, come and stay at my house.

LUKE (THE NARRATOR): When we were in Philippi, a slave girl who used to tell the future through an evil spirit followed behind Paul. She kept crying out:

GIRL: These men are servants of the Most High God! They're telling you how to be saved!

LUKE (THE NARRATOR): For many days she continued to do this. Becoming annoyed, Paul commanded the spirit:

PAUL: In the name of Jesus come out of her!

LUKE (THE NARRATOR): Immediately, the evil spirit left her. When her owners saw that they couldn't make money from her anymore, they grabbed Paul and Silas and dragged them before the city of officials. They claimed:

SLAVE OWNERS: These men are causing confusion in our city.

LUKE (THE NARRATOR): The officials had Paul and Silas beaten and thrown in jail. Placing them in the inner cell, the jailor fastened their feet in chains. About midnight, Paul and Silas were praying and singing to God. Suddenly, a huge earthquake shook the jail. All the prison doors were opened, and the prisoner's chains came loose. When the jailor woke up, he thought the prisoners had escaped.

PAUL: Don't worry! We're all here!

LUKE (THE NARRATOR): Rushing into the cell, the jailor fell at Paul and Silas' feet. Shaking, he asked:

JAILOR: What do I need to do to be saved?

SILAS: Believe in the Lord Jesus and you will be saved, you and your family.

LUKE (THE NARRATOR): Right away the jailor and his family were baptized. The next day Paul and Silas were released from jail.

In Jail

Paul was treated badly and put in jail in Philippi. It wasn't fair. But Paul didn't feel sorry for himself. He said he'd gladly give up anything if it could help him know Jesus more. Why? He realized Jesus is more wonderful than anything he could own or experience on earth (Phil. 3:8).

Thessalonica, Athens, and Corinth

Acts 17-18

LUKE (THE NARRATOR): Paul and Silas traveled to **Thessalonica**. For three weeks they spoke about Jesus in the synagogue.

PAUL: This Jesus I'm telling you about is the Christ, God's Chosen One.

LUKE (THE NARRATOR): Some Jews and a large number of non-Jews believed their message. Then other Jews became jealous. Gathering some troublemakers, they formed a mob and set the city in an uproar, shouting:

CROWD: These people have stirred up trouble all over the world! Now they've come here, too! They're acting against Caesar's decrees! They're saying there's another king named Jesus!

LUKE (THE NARRATOR): After the uproar, the believers sent Paul and Silas to **Berea**. Many of the Jews there believed Paul's message, along with a lot of important Greek women. When the Jews in Thessalonica heard that Paul was telling people in Berea the word of God, they came there and stirred up the crowds. Immediately, the believers sent Paul to **Athens** where he started telling people about Jesus.

PAUL: People of Athens, I see you're very religious. I found that you have an altar to "an unknown god." I'm going to tell you about this God. From one person, God made all the nations, deciding where and when they would live. He did this so we would search for God and find him. We are God's children. So, we shouldn't think of God like a gold or silver image made by humans. God won't judge you for not understanding him in the past. But now God commands everyone to change how they think about him. God has set a day when he's going to judge the world by a man he chose. He proved to everyone who this judge of the world is by raising him from the dead.

MAN IN ATHENS: I can't believe that.

WOMAN IN ATHENS: We want to hear you talk more about this another time.

LUKE (THE NARRATOR): After some people believed Paul's message in Athens, Paul traveled to **Corinth**. Every day Paul preached about Jesus. One night the Lord spoke to Paul in a vision.

JESUS: Don't be afraid. Speak up because I am with you. No one will harm you here. I have many people in this city.

LUKE (THE NARRATOR): For a year and a half Paul stayed in Corinth. He was very successful. Finally, Paul returned to Antioch where he had started his journey.

Review It!

Where did Paul and Silas go first? How did they know God wanted them to go to Macedonia?

What happened to Paul and Silas in Philippi?

How did people react to Paul's message in Thessalonica and Berea?

Remember It!

Learn these timeline events.

53. Philip baptizes an Ethiopian official
54. Saul persecutes the church
55. Gentiles believe in Jesus
56. Paul's First Journey—Cyprus' Governor believes
57. In Pisidian Antioch Paul teaches in the synagogue

Think About It!

Paul originally planned just to visit the places he had gone on his first journey. How were God's plans for Paul's journey larger than Paul's plans for it? What does that tell you about God's plans for your life?

Why did Paul and Silas stay in jail after the earthquake opened the doors and broke their chains? Why didn't they think the earthquake was God's way of releasing them from prison? What was more important to them than going free?

Everywhere Paul traveled people rejected him. How do you think Paul felt? What was more important to Paul than being popular?

Jesus is better than anything else.

Map It!

Dots show where cities are. Lines show where regions are. Label these places:

- Damascus
- Antioch
- Cyprus
- Antioch in Pisidia

- Iconium
- Lystra
- Derbe
- Cilicia
- Syria

- Troas
- Macedonia
- Philippi
- Thessalonica
- Berea

Draw a line connecting the places Paul visited on his second journey:

- Antioch
- Derbe
- Lystra
- Iconium

- Antioch in Pisidia
- Troas
- Philippi

- Thessalonica
- Berea
- Athens
- Corinth

© Master the Bible Ministries

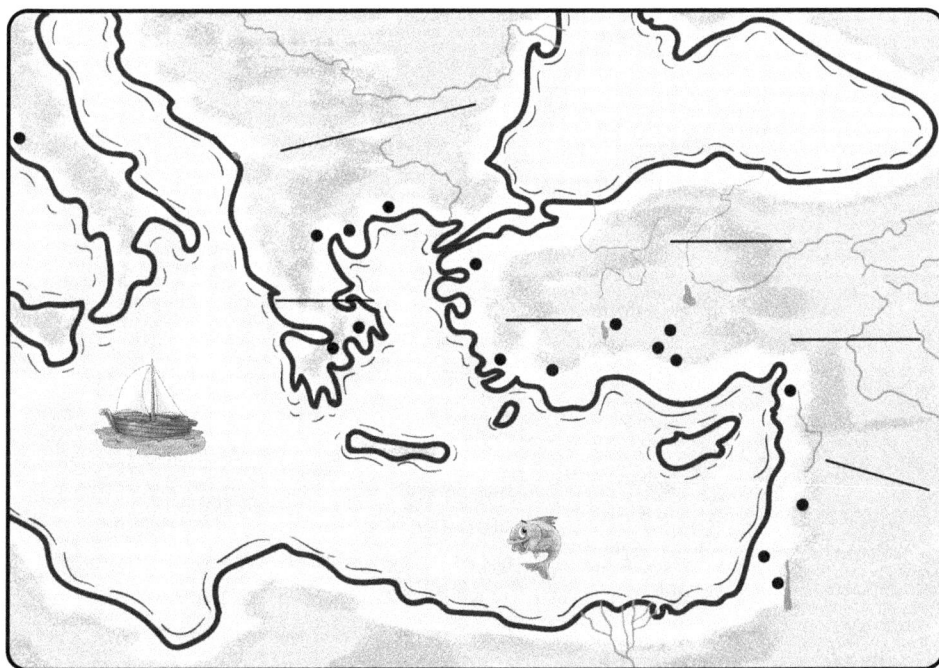

Answers in Appendix E Map 2

CHAPTER 11

Paul's Third Journey

Acts 19-21, Acts 28

DIRECTIONS: Read the story to yourself. Or read it as a family with each person reading a different part aloud. When you come to a place name in **bold**, draw a number 3 in that location on a map in Appendix E.

Ephesus
Acts 19

LUKE (THE NARRATOR): Paul arrived at **Ephesus** where he found some disciples.

PAUL: Did you receive the Holy Spirit when you believed?

BELIEVER: No, we haven't even heard that there is a Holy Spirit.

PAUL: What kind of baptism did you have?

BELIEVER: John's baptism.

PAUL: John's baptism was to let everyone know you had changed how you act and think. John told the people to believe in the one who was coming after him—Jesus.

LUKE (THE NARRATOR): After the people heard this, they were baptized in Jesus' name. When Paul put his hands on them, the Holy Spirit came on them. They heard God's words and spoke them. They also spoke in tongues, languages they had not known before. Altogether, there were about twelve men.

Mature

Paul did incredible miracles in Ephesus because he was spiritually mature. He didn't mature by trying hard to be good. Spiritual maturity comes by wanting and chasing after God more than other things.

Paul taught daily in the city for two years. Everyone in the entire province of **Asia** heard the word of the Lord. God did extraordinary miracles through Paul. When pieces of cloth that had touched Paul were taken to people who were sick, they were healed, and the evil spirits left.

Some Jews who traveled around casting out evil spirits tried to use the name of the Lord Jesus to set people free from evil spirits. They would say:

MAN: In the name of Jesus, whom Paul teaches about, I command you to come out.

LUKE (THE NARRATOR): Seven sons of an important Jewish priest named Sceva were doing this. One day, an evil spirit answered them:

EVIL SPIRIT: I know Jesus, and I know about Paul. But who are you?

LUKE (THE NARRATOR): Then the man with the evil spirit jumped on them and beat them all up. They ran out of the house naked. When people heard about this, they were afraid and honored the name of Jesus. Many of the believers publicly told people what they had done that was wrong. A lot of people who practiced magic brought their books and burned them publicly. The books were worth a lot of money. That's how the word of the Lord spread to a lot of places and grew in power.

PAUL: Now I want to go through **Macedonia** and **Greece**. Then I'll visit **Jerusalem**. After that I'll go to Rome.

LUKE (THE NARRATOR): But before Paul left Ephesus, a man named Demetrius got upset about the way of Jesus because fewer people were buying his idols of Artemus (who is also called Diana). Calling together all the people who made idols, he said:

DEMETRIUS: My friends, you know we make a lot of money from our business. You see how Paul teaches that gods made by human hands aren't gods. So many people have believed him that what we do is in danger of losing its good name. And the goddess Artemus will be robbed of her greatness!

LUKE (THE NARRATOR): Soon the city was in an uproar. For two hours they all shouted:

CROWD: Great is Artemus of the Ephesians!

LUKE (THE NARRATOR): A city official quieted the crowd and said:

OFFICIAL: If Demetrius has a complaint about someone, the courts are open. He can settle the matter in court. But there is no reason for all this trouble.

The Rest of the Journey and the End of Acts   Acts 20-21, Acts 28

LUKE (THE NARRATOR): When the riot ended, Paul decided to go to **Macedonia**. After traveling for several months through Macedonia and **Greece**, he got on a ship to sail toward **Jerusalem**. When the ship docked in **Troas**, Paul was talking until midnight with the believers. A young man named Eutychus was seated on a window in the third story. Becoming sleepy, he fell to the ground and died. Going down, Paul threw himself on him, hugged him, and said:

PAUL: Don't be afraid. He's alive!

Decisions

When things didn't go well in Jerusalem, Paul never worried about whether going there was a mistake. Because he was trying to follow God, Paul knew God would make any decision have a wonderful ending. And that's what happened. Paul's dream of preaching in Rome was fulfilled!

LUKE (THE NARRATOR): Then Paul went back upstairs and talked with them all night. Stopping along the way, we sailed back toward Jerusalem. In every town where we stopped, we found believers and visited with them. They told Paul:

BELIEVER: Don't go to Jerusalem!

LUKE (THE NARRATOR): When we came to **Caesarea**, we stayed with Philip (who told the Ethiopian about Jesus). He had four daughters who were prophetesses, meaning they spoke what they heard God saying. Then a prophet named Agabus visited. Taking Paul's belt, he tied his own hands and feet with it.

AGABUS: The Holy Spirit says that this what the Jews in Jerusalem will do to Paul. They'll hand him over to people who aren't Jews.

LUKE, PHILIP, AND PHILIP'S DAUGHTERS: Please don't go to Jerusalem!

PAUL: Why is everyone crying and making me sad?

I'm ready to be tied up. In fact, I'm ready to die in Jerusalem for the name of Jesus.

LUKE (THE NARRATOR): When we couldn't get Paul to change his mind we said:

LUKE, PHILIP, AND PHILIP'S DAUGHTERS: May what God wants to happen be done.

LUKE (THE NARRATOR): Paul was arrested in Jerusalem and put in jail for years. But God was kind to him and saved his life. Then Paul asked for Caesar to decide his lawsuit. So, Paul traveled with some others (including me) to **Rome**. God kept us safe even after a terrible storm wrecked the ship.

When we arrived in Rome, Paul told people there about Jesus, too. Everywhere he went, he told people about the kingdom of God and taught about the Lord Jesus Christ. He spoke and acted with boldness and didn't let anything stop him!

Review It!

How did Paul heal people in Ephesus?

Who caused a riot? Why?

What happened when a young man fell from the third story?

Did Paul decide to go to Jerusalem? What happened to him there?

Remember It!

SONGS: *Paul's First Journey and Paul's Second Journey*

Learn these timeline events.

58. Paul does miracles in Iconium
59. Paul is stoned in Lystra
60. Silas and Timothy join Paul's Second Journey
61. Lydia believes
62. Paul and Silas are jailed in Philippi

Think About It!

How did Jesus' followers grow from 12 (when Paul first arrived) to so many that the people who made idols were afraid of going out of business?

What was the climax (biggest, most important thing) of Paul's time in Ephesus? Why was it the climax?

How would you describe Paul's attitude and character based on the events in the second part of today's lesson?

I don't have to worry about whether I made a mistake. God can make any path I chose lead to a good ending.

Map It!

Dots show where cities are. Lines show where regions are. Label these places:

- Damascus
- Antioch
- Cyprus
- Antioch in Pisidia
- Iconium
- Lystra

- Derbe
- Cilicia
- Syria
- Troas
- Macedonia
- Philippi

- Thessalonica
- Berea
- Greece
- Athens
- Corinth
- Ephesus

Draw a line connecting the places Paul visited on his third journey:

- Antioch
- Derbe
- Lystra
- Iconium

- Antioch in Pisidia
- Ephesus
- Philippi

- Thessalonica
- Berea
- Athens
- Corinth

On the return journey:

- Berea
- Thessalonica

- Troas
- Caesarea

- Jerusalem

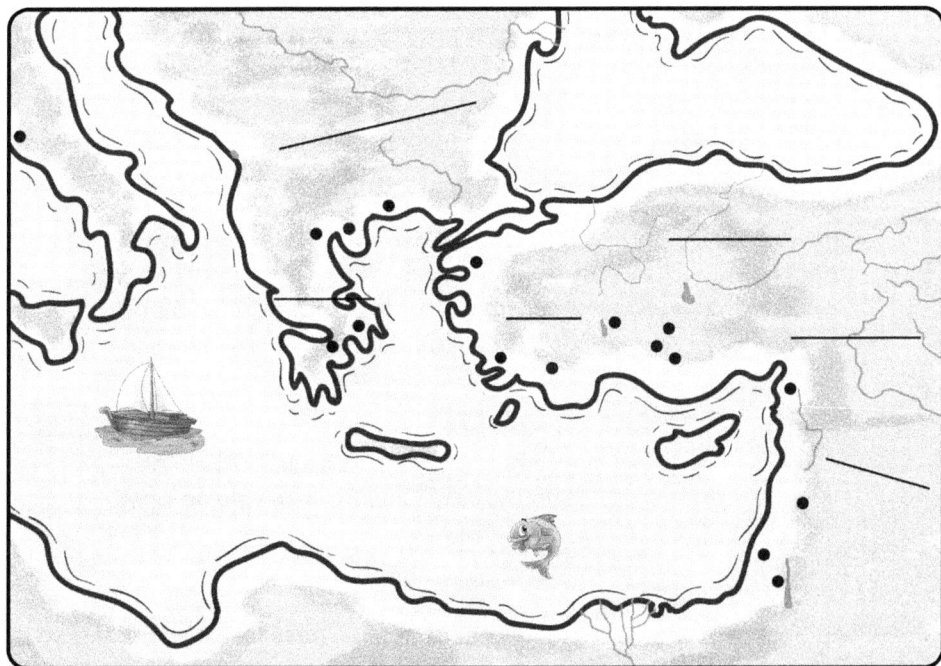

Answers in Appendix E Map 2

CHAPTER 12

Jesus' Greatest Teachings

Mark 12, Luke 10, 12, Matthew 6, 18

DIRECTIONS: Read the story to yourself. Or read it as a family with each person reading a different part aloud. When you come to a place name in **bold**, draw a sheep in that location on a map in Appendix E.

Greatest Commandment — Mark 12

NARRATOR: Jesus did miracles and preached everywhere he went. In this chapter, we're going to study some of Jesus' greatest teachings about how we should live our lives. Let's join Jesus in **Jerusalem**. He's walking in the temple courts, answering questions people are asking him.

TEACHER: Which of God's commandments is the most important?

JESUS: The most important one is this: Love the Lord your God with all your heart and with all your soul and with all your mind and with all your strength. The second most important commandment is this: Love your neighbor like you love yourself.

TEACHER: You're right. Loving God and loving others is more important than all the burnt offerings and sacrifices we could offer.

NARRATOR: When Jesus saw that he gave a wise answer, he said:

JESUS: You're not far from the kingdom of God.

Love

When we love people, we help them fulfill God's plan for their lives. That's one reason why loving God and others are the greatest commandments.

Greatest Commandment in Action

NARRATOR: Another time, someone who taught people God's law stood up to test Jesus.

TEACHER: Teacher, what do I need to do to have eternal life?

JESUS: What does God's law say?

TEACHER: Love the Lord your God with all your heart, with all your soul, and with all your strength, and with all your mind. And love your neighbor like you love yourself.

JESUS: That's the right answer. Do it and you will live.

NARRATOR: But the teacher of God's law wanted to feel like he was a good person. So, he asked Jesus:

TEACHER: Who is my neighbor?

JESUS: A man was going down from **Jerusalem** to **Jericho**. Robbers took his clothes, beat him up, and took off, leaving him almost dead. Now it so happened that a priest was going down that same road. When he saw the injured man, he walked by him on the other side of the road. Then a Levite, who serves in the temple, saw the man lying there, but walked by on the other side. Then a Samaritan, a person looked down on by the people living in Jerusalem, came to where the man was. Feeling sorry for him, he put bandages on his wounds, placed him on his own animal, and brought him to an inn. The next day he handed two silver coins to the innkeeper.

SAMARITAN: Take care of him while I'm gone. If you spend more than this, I'll pay you back when I return.

JESUS: Out of these three people, who was a neighbor to the man attacked by robbers?

TEACHER: The one who was kind to him.

JESUS: Go and do the same thing.

Impossible Test

The man thought of God like a teacher who graded his performance. He wanted to know if what he was doing was good enough to pass God's test. So, Jesus made the test so hard that it's impossible to pass. Jesus wanted him to know that God doesn't love us because we try hard. He loves us because he created us in his image—we're God's children.

JESUS: Don't look down on little children. I tell you, in heaven their angels always look at the face of my Father who is in heaven. What do you think? If someone owns a hundred sheep, and one wanders off, wouldn't he leave the ninety-nine on the mountain, and go search for the one who went astray? When he finds it, he celebrates more over that sheep than over the ninety-nine that didn't go astray. So, my father in heaven doesn't want even one of these little ones to be lost.

NARRATOR: Another time Jesus taught:

JESUS: Don't worry about what you will eat and what you will drink. All the nations of the world try hard to get these things. Your Father knows you need them. Try hard to get God's kingdom. Then these other things will be added to what you have, too.

Review It!

What is the most important commandment? Second most important?

Who is our neighbor?

What story did Jesus tell to show how much God loves people—even when they wander away from him?

What story did Jesus tell to show us that life is more than things we own?

Remember It!

SONGS: *Paul's Second Journey*

Learn these timeline events.

63. Thessalonians and Bereans believe despite opposition
64. Paul preaches about the Unknown God in Athens
65. Paul spends a year and a half in Corinth

Think About It!

Why is loving God with everything we are the most important commandment?

If Jesus had said that we just need to love kind people who are nice to us, would it be possible to do that? Why would Jesus make the commandments so difficult to keep? What does it tell us about our relationship with God?

Why is it foolish to trust in money to make us happy and safe?

God will take care of all my needs.

Map It!

Dots show where cities are. Lines show where regions are. Label these places:

- Damascus
- Antioch
- Cyprus
- Antioch in Pisidia
- Iconium
- Lystra

Answers in Appendix E Map 2

© Master the Bible Ministries

CHAPTER 13

Kingdom of Heaven

Matthew 6, 13

DIRECTIONS: Read the story to yourself. Or read it as a family with each person reading a different part aloud. When you come to a place name in **bold**, draw a seed in that location on a map in Appendix E.

What is the Kingdom of Heaven?

Matthew 6, 13

NARRATOR: Jesus taught about the kingdom of heaven everywhere he went. He taught us that in heaven, what God wants to happen is always done. That's why there is no sickness or disease or death in heaven. There is nothing bad in heaven because God's perfect will is always done. Jesus taught us to pray for God's kingdom to come to earth. He taught us to pray that what God wants to happen be done on earth like it's done in heaven. In **Galilee** Jesus gave these teachings.

Kingdom of Heaven

Imagine a place where what your heart really wants is satisfied. Imagine being fully like God—perfect and filled with glory. Imagine having "super-human" powers to walk on water, walk through walls, and change the substance of things. Imagine God's perfect will always happening. That's God's kingdom. It's worth giving up everything in this world to rule the universe with God.

JESUS: This is how you should pray: "Our Father, who lives in heaven, may your name be kept holy. May your kingdom come. May what you want to happen be done on earth like it's done in heaven."

NARRATOR: Jesus gave us pictures of what the kingdom of heaven is like by telling stories. Here are some of the stories he told about the kingdom of heaven.

JESUS: The kingdom of heaven is like a mustard seed that a man took and planted in his field. It's the smallest of all seeds. But when it has grown, it's the greatest of all the plants in a garden. Wild birds even come and make nests in its branches. The kingdom of heaven is like yeast that a woman mixed with a large amount of flour—enough flour to feed a hundred people. She mixed the yeast into the flour until all the dough had risen.

NARRATOR: Jesus taught us that the kingdom of heaven starts small but grows large—just like a mustard seed or a small amount of yeast. We enter God's kingdom by making Jesus our king, by doing what he wants us to do. Our decision to follow Jesus will grow until Jesus becomes the biggest, most important part of our lives. Here are two more stories Jesus told about the kingdom of heaven:

JESUS: The kingdom of heaven is like a treasure that a person found and hid in a field. Because he was so happy, he sold everything he had to buy the field. The kingdom of heaven is also like a trader looking for beautiful pearls. When he found a very valuable pearl, he sold everything he had to buy it.

NARRATOR: The kingdom of heaven is so valuable, just like a treasure or an expensive jewel. The people who find God's kingdom gladly get rid of everything else in their lives so that they can have it.

How do I Grow in the Kingdom of Heaven?   Matthew 13

JESUS: A farmer went out to plant seeds. As he scattered his seeds, some seeds fell on the path and the birds came and ate them. Other seeds fell on soil with a lot of rocks in it. They grew up quickly because the soil wasn't deep. But when the sun came out, they were burnt up. They didn't have deep enough roots, so they withered. Other seeds fell in the thorns. When those seeds began to grow, the thorns choked them. But other seeds fell in good soil. They produced grain. Some made 100 times more grain than was planted. Others produced sixty or thirty times as much.

DISCIPLES: What does this story mean? Can you explain it to us?

JESUS: When someone hears a teaching about the kingdom of heaven and doesn't understand it, the evil one comes and snatches away what was planted in that person's heart. This is the seed that fell on the path. The seed that fell on the rocky ground is the person who hears a teaching and immediately is excited about it. But because there is no root, it doesn't last long. When it becomes difficult to follow the teaching or when people treat them badly for doing what they learned, the person immediately falls away.

DISCIPLES: What is the seed that fell in the thorns?

JESUS: The seed that fell in the thorns is the person who hears a teaching, but the person is concerned with the things of this world and with becoming rich. These concerns choke the teaching so it doesn't produce anything in their lives.

Growing Seeds

To grow a teaching about God's kingdom in our lives, first we need to make sure we understand it. Ask someone if you have questions. Second, "water" it by thinking about it or listening to more teaching about it again and again. Third, pull out weeds that try to choke the teaching. Finally, try to do it. Like a plant, we'll start small. But we can grow to do mighty things.

DISCIPLES: What is the seed that fell on good soil?

JESUS: The seed that fell on good soil is the person who hears a teaching and understands it. This person produces fruit—100, 60, or 30 times what was planted.

NARRATOR: Every time you hear someone teach about God's kingdom, it's like a seed is planted inside you. That seed can grow into something big and wonderful. Or it may not. To have a teaching about God grow inside you, you need to treat it like you would a little seed that you want to grow. Give attention to it and care for it. Then the teaching will grow inside you, and you will be able to help many, many more people with what you learned.

Review It!

What did Jesus teach us to pray about the kingdom of heaven?

What seed did Jesus compare the kingdom of heaven to?
What baking ingredient did he say the kingdom of heaven is like?

In the stories about the treasure and the pearl, how did the person feel about selling everything they had for the kingdom of God?

What story did Jesus tell to show us how to grow stronger in the kingdom of heaven?

Remember It!

SONGS: *Paul's Third Journey*

Learn these timeline events.

66. Paul sparks a revival then riot in Ephesus
67. Paul raises Eutychus from the dead
68. Agabus warns Paul about going to Jerusalem

What is the kingdom of heaven? How would you explain it to someone?

Why would someone happily give everything they own to enter God's kingdom?

Have you ever tried to grow a plant? How is growing a teaching inside you like growing a plant? What do you need to do to grow one of Jesus' teachings inside you so that it gives you a big crop?

I can pray for God's perfect will to be done in my life just like it would be done if I lived in heaven.

Map It!

Dots show where cities are. Lines show where regions are. Label these places:

- Damascus
- Antioch
- Cyprus
- Antioch in Pisidia
- Iconium
- Lystra

- Derbe
- Cilicia
- Syria
- Troas
- Macedonia
- Philippi

Answers in Appendix E Map 2

© Master the Bible Ministries

CHAPTER 14

Grace and Gifts

Romans, 1-2 Corinthians

DIRECTIONS: Read the story to yourself. Or read it as a family with each person reading a different part aloud. When you come to a place name in **bold**, draw an eye in that location on a map in Appendix E.

How do you have a good relationship with God?

Romans 2-4

PAUL: I, Paul, am writing to the people God loves in **Rome**. There are some things that I want you to understand. God will reward everyone for what they've done on the day he judges the world. He'll give eternal life to the people who keep doing good. These people seek glory and honor and life that never ends. But people who do evil will have trouble and difficulty.

ROMAN PERSON: How can we have eternal life? We know the Bible says, "No one is righteous, not even one person. No one understands or seeks God."

PAUL: You're right that God doesn't give people eternal life because they do enough righteous things. It's impossible to become righteous in God's eyes by keeping a list of rules. But now God has revealed a way to become righteous without following a list of rules—the righteousness that comes through Jesus. Everyone has sinned and doesn't measure up to God's glory. But now everyone can be forgiven and declared righteous by believing in Jesus. It's a free gift. God doesn't give eternal life to you because you deserve it but because of his grace.

ROMAN PERSON: If someone works and is paid, then that's not grace. They deserve to be paid for working.

PAUL: That's right. But you are saved by grace, through faith in Jesus. It's not something you earn or deserve.

It's a gift you accept from God. What happened with our ancestors Abraham and Sarah shows you how grace works.

ABRAHAM: God, you promised me a son, but Sarah and I are old now and your promise hasn't come true.

GOD: Look up at the stars. Count them if you can. That's how many people will call you their ancestor.

ABRAHAM: I believe you.

GOD: I consider you righteous because you believed what I said.

PAUL: God called Abraham "righteous" not because Abraham and Sarah were able to do something great for God. He called them "righteous" because they believed what God told them even though it seemed impossible. This story shows us that believing in Jesus is what makes us righteous.

Righteous

God considered Abraham righteous because he believed what God said. God considers you righteous when you believe what he said about Jesus. (There's nothing else you have to do to be righteous.)

Your Gifts from God

1 Corinthians 12

PAUL: I, Paul, am writing this letter to God's church in **Corinth**. I want you to know about gifts God gives your spirit. The Holy Spirit gives every believer spiritual gifts so they can use them to help other people. The Spirit gives one person something wise to say or teach. To another person, the Spirit gives knowledge to share that they didn't know on their own. To someone else, the Spirit gives faith, and to another he gives gifts of healing. To someone else, the Spirit gives the ability to do miracles, and to another the ability to hear God's words and speak them. To someone else, the Spirit gives the ability to tell which kind of spirit is working. To another person, he gives the ability to speak different kinds of languages they didn't know before. To someone else he gives the ability to tell people what was said in those languages. It is one and the same Spirit giving people gifts as he decides.

CORINTHIAN PERSON: What if the gifts I get don't seem as important as someone else's gifts? Does that mean I'm less important?

PAUL: Every part of your body is important. Does your foot say:

FOOT: I'm not a hand, so I'm not important.

PAUL: Or, does your ear say:

EAR: I'm not an eye, so I'm not important.

PAUL: If your whole body were an eye, how would you hear? And if your whole body were an ear, how would you smell? God has placed each part of your body just as he decided they should go. So, your eye can't say to the hand:

EYE: I don't need you.

PAUL: And your head can't say to your foot:

HEAD: I don't need you.

Gifted

God gave gifts to your spirit so you could help other people through his supernatural power. How do you figure out what your gifts are? Ask God to show you. Do what you love doing. Try new things. You can also ask God for the gifts you want. Then try to do them.

PAUL: Actually, the parts of our body that seem weaker we can't live without. In the same way, God has put all his people together so that nothing divides us, and we're all concerned for each other. You are Christ's body. You are each part of it. God has placed first in the church apostles. Second, he gave us prophets who hear God's words and speak them. Third, he gave teachers. Then he gave people who do miracles. He also gave us people who have gifts of healing, people who help in different ways, people who are different kinds of leaders, and people who can speak in different kinds of languages they didn't learn.

CORINTHIAN PERSON: Is everyone an apostle? Is everyone a prophet or teacher? Is everyone a miracle worker?

PAUL: Not everyone is placed in the position of apostle or prophet or teacher or miracle worker.

CORINTHIAN PERSON: Does everyone have gifts of healing? Does everyone speak in languages they didn't learn? Does everyone explain the meaning of those languages?

PAUL: Not everyone has gifts of healing or speaks in languages they didn't learn. And not everyone explains the meaning of those languages. But you should strongly desire the greater gifts.

Review It!

Who wrote the letters to Rome and Corinth?

Why did God count Abraham and Sarah righteous?

What are some of the gifts Holy Spirit gives God's children?

Are there any gifts that aren't important? What did Paul compare spiritual gifts to? Are there parts of your body you don't need?

Remember It!

SONGS: *How does Acts End?*

Learn these timeline events.

69. Paul is arrested in the temple and spends two years in jail
70. Paul appeals to Caesar and is shipwrecked
71. Paul preaches in Rome
72. Apostles and their helpers write Letters
73. John writes Revelation

Think About It!

Is it true that no one is righteous? Why do we have to be saved by grace?

What is grace? If doing good things doesn't save us, then why should we do good?

If every spiritual gift is important, why does Paul tell us to strongly desire the greater gifts? What are the greater gifts? If he tells us to desire them does that mean God would give them to us?

I am important, wanted, and needed in God's kingdom.

Dots show where cities are. Lines show where regions are. Label these places:

- Damascus
- Antioch
- Cyprus
- Antioch in Pisidia
- Iconium
- Lystra
- Derbe
- Cilicia
- Syria

- Troas
- Macedonia
- Philippi
- Thessalonica
- Berea
- Greece
- Athens
- Corinth
- Ephesus

© Master the Bible Ministries

Answers in Appendix E Map 2

CHAPTER 15

How to Grow Spiritually

Galatians, Ephesians, Philippians, Colossians, 1-2 Thessalonians

DIRECTIONS: Read the story to yourself. Or read it as a family with each person reading a different part aloud. When you come to a place name in **bold**, draw a chair in that location on a map in Appendix E.

Where is Jesus now?

Ephesians 1-2

PAUL: I, Paul, am writing to the saints in **Ephesus**. God has blessed us with every spiritual blessing from heaven because we belong to Jesus. He chose us in Christ before he created the world to be holy and without blame in his eyes. He loved us. I pray that God would give you the Spirit of wisdom and revelation so that you can see things from heaven's point of view. I pray that you would grow to know God better and better. I pray that you would know the wonderful things God has prepared for us. It's full of glory. I pray that you would understand how great his power is for us who believe.

Seated in Heaven

Jesus is in heaven above every power in earth or heaven. Guess who is seated next to Jesus? You are! God gave you a seat next to Jesus in heaven where you can rule with him.

He showed this power when he raised Jesus from the dead and had him sit at God's right hand in heaven.

EPHESIAN PERSON: Where is Jesus now?

PAUL: Jesus is at God's right hand in heaven. He's far above everyone who rules and has authority on earth or in the spiritual world. He is far above all spiritual powers and all kings. He is far above every title or name that can be given in this world and in the world that is coming.

EPHESIAN PERSON: What is under Jesus' rule?

PAUL: God put everything under Jesus' rule. God gave Jesus to the church as the head over all things.

EPHESIAN PERSON: Why did God save us?

PAUL: Because God loves us so much, he saved us by his grace. Jesus died. We were also dead in our spirits because of the wrong things we had done. But God made us alive with Jesus because he loves us so much. He raised us up with Jesus and gave us seats next to Jesus in heaven.

EPHESIAN PERSON: What does God think of me?

PAUL: We are God's special work.

How do I grow up spiritually?
Colossians 3

PAUL: I, Paul, am writing to the saints in **Colossae**. Keep thinking about things in heaven and not things on earth. Everyone will know how full of glory Jesus is. When that happens, everyone will see how full of glory you are, too. So put to death anything in your nature that belongs to the earth and not heaven. Don't desire evil things.

COLOSSIAN PERSON: We used to do bad things.

PAUL: Before you knew Jesus, you did bad things. But now you should take off being angry, telling lies, and doing evil. Don't say bad things about God, and don't let any bad language come out of your mouths.

COLOSSIAN PERSON: If we have done these bad things, what does God think of us?

PAUL: You are God's chosen people. He loves you so much and has made you holy. You should take off evil things because they don't show who you are.

COLOSSIAN PERSON: So we should take off these bad things like we take off dirty clothes. What should we put on instead?

PAUL: Clothe yourselves with tender concern for each other from deep in your hearts. Then add kindness, humility, gentleness, and patience. Forgive each other just as Jesus forgave you. Above everything else, put on love, which ties all these good things together.

COLOSSIAN PERSON: After we dress ourselves with all these virtues, what should we do?

PAUL: Be full of the peace that Jesus gives you. Be thankful. Let Christ's word live in you like a spiritual treasure. You should teach each other. Sing to God. And whatever you say or do, do it all in the name of the Lord Jesus.

What is the best thing ever?

Philippians 3

PAUL: I'm now writing a letter to the saints of Jesus who are in **Philippi**.

PHILIPPIAN PERSON: Paul, when you were with us, you were beaten and put in jail for following Jesus. You've suffered a lot of other things in order to follow Jesus. Why did you do that?

Changing Clothes

Our spirits are like Jesus—full of glory. We should put off our "old clothes"—anger, lies, unclean things—because they don't fit with who we are. We should put on our "new clothes"— kindness, humility, patience, and love. Then what our spirits are wearing will match who we really are.

PAUL: I used to have a lot of things I thought I could brag about. But now I realize that knowing Jesus is a lot more valuable than anything else I could have. Because knowing Jesus is so much better than anything else, I will give up anything so that I can gain Christ. The things I gave up seem like garbage to me. Compared to knowing Jesus, everything else seems like something you would want to immediately throw away.

PHILIPPIAN PERSON: Is there a reward for knowing Jesus?

PAUL: Yes, God gives us a prize for knowing Jesus. There are crowns and rewards and treasures in heaven. Some prizes and crowns God will award to us when Jesus appears again.

Review It!

Where is Jesus now?

Why did God save you? What does God think of you?

To grow up spiritually, what do we need to take off? What do we need to put on?

What would Paul give up in order to know Jesus better?

Remember It!

SONGS: *Paul's First Journey and Paul's Second Journey*

Learn six of the 12 Apostles

- Peter
- Andrew
- James
- John
- Philip
- Bartholomew

Think About It!

Paul says that Jesus is seated in heaven above every authority and power. Where does Paul say we are seated? Who has more power than we do? Who has less power?

How can we put off bad things without trusting in a list of rules to make us holy? How can we keep God the one who makes us holy—and still try hard ourselves?

What have you given up so that you could know Jesus better? Was it worth it? Do you want to know Jesus in such a way that everything else seems like garbage?

I will rule with Jesus.

Map It!

Dots show where cities are. Lines show where regions are. Label these places:

- Damascus
- Antioch
- Cyprus
- Antioch in Pisidia
- Iconium
- Lystra
- Derbe
- Cilicia
- Syria
- Troas
- Macedonia
- Philippi

- Thessalonica
- Berea
- Greece
- Athens
- Corinth
- Ephesus
- Galatia
- Jerusalem
- Rome
- Crete
- Caesarea

© Master the Bible Ministries

Answers in Appendix E Map 2

CHAPTER 16

How to Live God's Plan for Your Life

1-2 Timothy, Hebrews

DIRECTIONS: Read the story to yourself. Or read it as a family with each person reading a different part aloud. When you come to a place name in **bold**, draw a coin in that location on a map in Appendix E.

How should a young person act? 1 Timothy 2, 4-5, 2 Timothy 1-2

PAUL: I, Paul, am writing this letter to Timothy, my son in the faith. When I left for **Macedonia**, I told you to stay in **Ephesus** to teach people there. First, I want all of you pray for everybody. Pray for our leaders so we can live in peace.

TIMOTHY: I'm young, and sometimes I'm afraid to use the gift God gave me.

PAUL: Don't let anyone look down on you because you're young. Set an example for them in how you talk and how you act. Show them how much you love and how faithful and pure you are.

TIMOTHY: Sometimes I forget about the spiritual gift God gave me.

Friends

Who my friends are matters. Friends can draw me closer to God—or farther from him.

PAUL: Don't forget to use the spiritual gift you have. Remember how God gave it to you when the elders laid their hands on you. Remember how God made clear that he gave you the gift because he spoke to people about you. They shared what they heard God saying. Think carefully about these things. Give everything you have to them so everyone can see your progress. Stir up the gift God gave you until it becomes a huge fire inside you again. God didn't give you a spirit that's afraid. He gave you a spirit that has power, love, and good judgment about what to do.

TIMOTHY: How should I act around other people?

PAUL: Don't speak to an older man with harsh words. Urge him like he's your father. Encourage younger men like they're your brothers. Talk to older women like mothers, and younger women like sisters. Be totally pure in how you treat them.

TIMOTHY: A lot of people my age are doing things they shouldn't do. They want me to join them.

PAUL: Run away from evil things young people want to do, and run after doing what is right. Pursue faith, love and peace. Be friends with people who call on the Lord with a pure heart.

Be happy with what you have and don't give up
1 Timothy 6, 2 Timothy 3

PAUL: I'll tell you what a huge profit is. Living a life that respects God and being happy with what you have is worth a lot. We didn't bring anything into the world. We're not going to take anything out of it, either. So, what good does it really do us to make a lot of money? But if we have food and shelter, we'll be satisfied with that.

TIMOTHY: Some people really want to become rich.

PAUL: People who long to be rich stumble into a trap. They trip because they strongly desire foolish things. Loving money is a root of all evils. Some people who have followed their desire for money have been led away from the faith. They've deeply wounded themselves with many sorrows.

TIMOTHY: I understand that it's foolish to love money and long to be rich. But some people are rich. Is that okay?

PAUL: Tell people who are rich in this present world not to think they are better than others. Tell them not to trust in riches. Wealth is uncertain. They should trust in God who richly gives us everything to enjoy.

TIMOTHY: Is there anything else I should tell rich people to do?

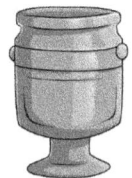

PAUL: Tell them to be rich in doing good things for people. They should be generous and ready to share. When they do this, they will save up a treasure for themselves in heaven.

TIMOTHY: What can help me when I face difficult things?

PAUL: Ever since you were a small baby, you have known the holy writings. They have the power to make you wise so you can be saved from danger. You're rescued by believing in Jesus Christ.

From the Book of Hebrews   Hebrews 6, Hebrews 12

BELIEVER: Some people want to leave their faith when they are mistreated for following Jesus.

HEBREW'S AUTHOR: We really want each of you to show the same commitment until the end. You want to see what Jesus promised you to happen. Stay excited until the end. Be like the people who inherited the promises because they had faith. They suffered difficult things with patience.

BELIEVER: I know that Jesus entered heaven after he rose from the dead.

HEBREW'S AUTHOR: Yes, he's there now in God's presence to argue for us before God. Think about Jesus. He suffered patiently when sinful people treated him badly. Remember what Jesus went through so you won't grow tired and give up.

Hard Things

Sometimes God allows me to go through something difficult so my character can become like his. So, I can be excited about going through something difficult. I know it will make my life into something wonderful that it couldn't be without the difficult thing.

BELIEVER: What can I gain for suffering for Jesus?

HEBREW'S AUTHOR: God disciplines everyone he loves and accepts as a child. When you suffer, God is treating you like true children. Discipline isn't fun. It's painful at the time. But later it brings peace and righteousness to your life. People who suffer for Jesus gain peace and righteousness in this world. In the world to come, they will rule with Jesus.

Review It!

Who wrote to Timothy? Where was Timothy a church leader?

What were some things Paul told Timothy to do?

Should people try to become rich? If people are rich, what should they do?

What would help Timothy when he faced difficult things?

Remember It!

SONGS: *Paul's First Journey and Paul's Second Journey*

Learn the other six of the 12 Apostles

- Thomas
- Matthew
- James son of Alphaeus
- Thaddaeus
- Simon the Zealot
- Judas Iscariot (replaced by Matthias)

What did Paul tell Timothy to do when he felt afraid or forgot to use his spiritual gift? Why would those things help?

Why is wanting to become rich a trap? What is true wealth? How can we use our money so it builds true wealth?

Has anyone ever treated you poorly because you believe in Jesus? How can remembering Jesus' suffering help you? What did Jesus gain from his suffering?

I can be rich for eternity when I share what I have now.

Dots show where cities are. Lines show where regions are. Label these places:

- Nazareth
- Bethlehem
- Cana
- Jerusalem
- Jordan River
- Dead Sea
- Capernaum

- Galilee
- Sea of Galilee
- Bethsaida
- Caesarea-Philippi
- Judea
- Samaria
- Bethany

Answers in Appendix E Map 1

CHAPTER 17

Important Truths to Live By

James, 1-2 Peter, 1-3 John, Jude

DIRECTIONS: Read the story to yourself. Or read it as a family with each person reading a different part aloud. James may have written from **Jerusalem.** John may have written from **Ephesus.** Draw a pen in those locations on a map in Appendix E.

Letter from James

James 1, 4-5

JAMES: I am writing this letter because I have a lot of important things I want you to remember. Here's one of them: When you're tempted, don't say:

Powerful Prayers

Our prayers can be as powerful as anyone's in the Bible—even Elijah whose prayers controlled the weather! Any believer can have miraculous results to our prayers.

BELIEVER: God is tempting me.

JAMES: God can't be tempted by evil, and he can't tempt anyone. The scripture says:

BELIEVER: God opposes people who are proud, but he gives grace to the humble.

JAMES: So, do what God wants you to do. Oppose the devil, and he will run away from you. Come close to God, and he will come close to you.

SICK PERSON: What should I do if I'm sick?

JAMES: Are you suffering? You should pray. Are you happy? You should sing praises. Are you sick? You should call for the elders of the church. They'll pray for you and anoint you with oil in the name of the Lord.

The prayer of faith will save the sick person. The Lord will raise him up. So, tell each other what you've done wrong. And pray for each other so you can be healed. The prayer of a righteous person is very powerful.

BELIEVER: How powerful can one person's prayers be?

JAMES: Elijah was a regular person, just like us. He prayed that it wouldn't rain. And there was no rain for three and a half years! Then he prayed again, and it rained and brought a harvest.

Letters from Peter, John, and Jude

1 Peter 2, 2 Peter 1-3, 1 John 1-2, 3 John, Jude

Peter's Letters

PETER: I, Peter, am writing this letter to believers in **Galatia**, **Asia**, and places near there. God chose you to be his family, his group of priests, his holy nation. He picked you to be his own people so you could tell about how wonderful he is. He called you out of darkness into his amazing light.

BELIEVER: Did you really see everything about Jesus that you've told us about?

PETER: Yes. We didn't make up clever stories about Jesus when we told you about his power and about how he is going to return. We saw with our own eyes everything we told you. Pay attention to the prophecies about him. They will light up your understanding just like a light shines in the darkness. When the sun rises, the darkness will completely disappear. Then you'll see and understand everything clearly.

1 John

JOHN: I, John, am writing this letter to people who believe in Jesus. Walk in the light like God is in the light. If we do, we have close relationships with others. And the blood of Jesus Christ God's Son cleans us from all sin.

BELIEVER: What should I do when I sin?

JOHN: If you sin, we have someone who speaks for us before the Father—Jesus Christ the Righteous One. He himself paid for our sins. So don't worry. God will listen to Jesus and forgive your sins.

BELIEVER: How can I know God loves me?

JOHN: God loves us with such a great love that he calls us his children. And that's what we are! Just like children are like their parents, we know that we will be like him forever.

3 John

JOHN: I, John, am writing another letter to my good friend Gaius. I know that your spiritual life is going well. I pray that your body would be healthy, too.

GAIUS: Did the brothers in our faith come to you and tell you how I'm doing?

God's Child

Sometimes children look like their parents. Sometimes they act like their parents or have abilities like their parents' abilities. You are God's child. Your spirit looks like his spirit. Your spirit is holy like God's Spirit. You have God's abilities inside you.

JOHN: Yes, the brothers told me you're still living by the truth. I was so happy to hear that! Dear friend, you show that you are faithful to God by supporting our brothers and sisters who travel to teach about Jesus. Please again give them everything they need for their journey. Do it how you think God would. When you support people like that, it's like you are joining them on their journey. You become a fellow worker with them.

Jude

JUDE: I, Jude, am writing this letter to believers. You are wrapped in God's love and guarded by Jesus Christ. Dear friends, I have been so excited to write to you about how God has saved us. But now I feel like I need to write a different message. I need to encourage you to hold to the faith that God gave us. We're supposed to keep it pure and pass it along to others.

BELIEVER: I know some people say they are teaching us the truth, but they're not. How can we tell if someone isn't keeping the faith pure?

JUDE: People who make fun of the pure faith will be driven by their own selfish desires. They will cause divisions and will live like what's in the natural world is most important. They won't have God's Spirit living in them.

BELIEVER: We aren't like that. We keep ourselves in God's love.

JUDE: Yes. God is able to keep you from falling. He makes you stand in his glorious presence full of joy and without having anything wrong with you. He's the only God, and he saved us through Jesus Christ our Lord. To him belong glory, majesty, power, and authority—before all time, now and forever! Amen.

Review It!

Who wrote the letters in this chapter's lesson?

Is it okay to say bad things about someone? Why does James say it's not okay?

How do we know that God forgives us when we sin? What did John say?

Jude said God is able to keep us from falling. What else did he say God did for us?

Remember It!

SONGS: *Paul's First Journey and Paul's Second Journey*

Learn the names of Jesus' women leaders.

- Mary Magdalene
- Joanna
- Susanna
- Mary the mother of James and Joses
- Mary the wife of Clopas
- Salome

Think About It!

Peter said that he saw with his own eyes everything he taught about Jesus. Why do you think it's important that New Testament teaching is based on what eyewitnesses (people who saw things with their own eyes) saw and heard?

Have you ever prayed for something and seen a wonderful result? James says a regular person can have amazing results from their prayers. Why do you think that's true? Why don't we have to be special or super holy to see miraculous results when we pray?

What does Jude tell us to look for to see if someone is teaching us what is right? Why are those things a good test for truth?

God helps me overcome when I'm tempted to do evil.

Map It!

Dots show where cities are. Lines show where regions are. Label these places:

- Damascus
- Antioch
- Cyprus
- Antioch in Pisidia
- Iconium
- Lystra
- Derbe
- Cilicia
- Syria
- Troas
- Macedonia
- Philippi

- Thessalonica
- Berea
- Greece
- Athens
- Corinth
- Ephesus
- Galatia
- Jerusalem
- Rome
- Crete
- Caesarea

Answers in Appendix E Map 2

CHAPTER 18

God's Plan to Bring Heaven to Earth

Revelation

DIRECTIONS: Read the story to yourself. Or read it as a family with each person reading a different part aloud. When you come to a place name in **bold**, draw a cloud in that location on a map in Appendix E.

John Goes to Heaven   Revelation 1-11

JOHN: God sent an angel to me to show me things about Jesus Christ. The first thing I saw was Jesus himself! He told me to write the visions I saw in a book and send it to seven churches in the area where I was living.

JESUS: Write to the angels of the churches in **Ephesus**, Smyrna, Pergamum, Thyatira, Sardis, Philadelphia, and Laodicea. Tell them I know what they're doing right and what has pleased me. Tell them to put away the bad things some of them are doing so I don't have to come against the people who are sinning. To everyone who overcomes I'll give eternal life. They will rule the nations with me, sitting beside me on my throne.

VOICE: Come up here so I can show you what must happen.

JOHN: I saw a throne in heaven with someone sitting on it! The one sitting there looked like jewels. There was a rainbow that looked like an emerald circling the throne.

Twenty-four elders sat on thrones in a circle around God's throne. They were wearing white clothes and had gold crowns on their heads.

In front of the throne was something that looked like a sea of glass. In the center around the throne were four living creatures, looking like a lion, an ox, a person, and an eagle. All day and night they said:

LIVING CREATURES: Holy, Holy, Holy is the Lord, God, the All-Powerful! He was and he is, and he will come!

JOHN: When the living creatures worship God, the elders throw themselves down before God's throne and lay down their crowns, saying:

ELDERS: You are worthy, our Lord and God, to receive glory and honor and power because you created everything!

JOHN: Then I saw a scroll sealed with seven seals in God's right hand. A powerful angel proclaimed:

ANGEL: Who is worthy to open the scroll and break its seals?

JOHN: No one in heaven or earth was able to open the scroll. I started crying because no one could open the scroll.

ELDER: Stop crying! Look! Jesus has won! He can open the scroll and its seven seals.

Heaven

God wanted John to come up to heaven to see what was going to happen. God wants to share things with me, too. Like John, God can show me things about Jesus in heaven.

JOHN: Then the elders and living creatures sang a new song:

ELDERS AND LIVING CREATURES: You are worthy to take the scroll and open its seals. You paid your life to buy people for God. They come from every nation and tribe and language. You have made them a kingdom and priests to serve God. They will rule on the earth.

JOHN: I watched as Jesus opened each of the seven seals. I also watched as seven angels blew trumpets. With each seal and trumpet, a judgment of God was released! There were wars and earthquakes and famines. God was cleaning the earth from evil!

JOHN: Then I saw Satan's plan for earth unfold. Satan tried to rule the whole earth through a man. He set up a government that ruled every people group on earth. He even made everyone get a mark on their forehead or hand. Without this mark, no one could buy or sell things.

ANGEL: If anyone worships Satan's man or gets his mark on their forehead or hand, they will be punished just like Satan.

JOHN: Then in heaven I saw the people who had conquered Satan's man, rejoicing and singing praises to God. Then seven angels with seven bowls appeared.

ANGEL: I'll show you how God will destroy Satan's rule of the earth. His system has controlled the earth's governments and economies. A government will rise up to rule the earth. Everyone whose name isn't written in the book of life will be amazed by it. Several nations will join together to give their authority to the new government. They will make war on Jesus, but Jesus will conquer them because he's the Lord of lords and King of kings.

JOHN: Then I heard another angel shout:

ANGEL: Fallen! Fallen is the system Satan used to rule the earth! Kings and traders became wealthy and powerful from its rich, ungodly living.

VOICE: Come out of Satan's system, my people! So, you won't take part in its sins and so you won't be punished along with it.

God's Plan

God wants me to understand his plans for the world. He wants me to be part of what he's doing in the earth right now.

JOHN: In a single hour Satan's economic system fell. Through it he had deceived the world. Then I saw heaven opened, and Jesus came riding on a white horse. Heaven's armies, dressed in white clothes, were riding behind him on white horses. Jesus will rule the nations. Then Satan's man and the armies of the earth gathered to fight Jesus and his army. Jesus won.

Then I saw a great white throne and one sitting on it. And I saw everyone who had died standing before the throne to be judged. The book of life was opened. If anyone's name was not found written in the book of life, that person was thrown into the lake of fire.

Then I saw the new **Jerusalem** coming down from heaven. And a voice from the throne said:

VOICE: Look! God will live with people. They will be his people, and God himself will be with them. He will wipe every tear from their eyes. Death will not exist anymore— or sadness or crying or pain. The old things are gone.

JESUS: Yes, I am coming soon!

Review It!

What cities did Jesus have letters for?

When John saw heaven, who was in God's throne room? Where were they standing? What were they doing?

Who tried to rule heaven and earth instead of Jesus? What were some parts of his plan to rule the earth? Did it work?

How would you describe the new Jerusalem that comes down from heaven? Who will live there? What will it be like?

Remember It!

SONGS: *Who Helped Spread the Good News?*

Learn the names of those who helped to spread the Good News.

- Paul
- Barnabus
- Timothy
- Titus
- John
- Mark
- Silas

- Luke
- Priscilla
- Aquila
- Apollos
- Peter
- Aristarchus
- Tychicus

Think About It!

Revelation describes how the earth will shift from being ruled by an ungodly system to being ruled by the kingdom of heaven. Why does part of that process involve judging evil? Why can't God just erase evil? Why do the seals, trumpets, and bowls bring natural disasters and other difficult things?

Heaven urged people to come out of Satan's system so we wouldn't be judged with it. What is Satan's system? How can we come out of it?

Who was amazed by the government Satan's man set up? Why do you think they were deceived by it? What can keep you from being tricked?

God created me to be like him and rule with him forever.

Map It!

Print larger blank maps from the website. Label these places:

- Nazareth
- Bethlehem
- Cana
- Jerusalem
- Jordan River
- Dead Sea
- Capernaum
- Galilee
- Sea of Galilee
- Bethsaida
- Caesarea
- Philippi
- Judea
- Samaria
- Bethany

Answers in Appendix E Map 1

© Master the Bible Ministries

Label these places:

- Damascus
- Antioch
- Cyprus
- Antioch in Pisidia
- Iconium
- Lystra
- Derbe
- Cilicia
- Syria
- Troas
- Macedonia
- Philippi

- Thessalonica
- Berea
- Greece
- Athens
- Corinth
- Ephesus
- Galatia
- Jerusalem
- Rome
- Crete
- Caesarea

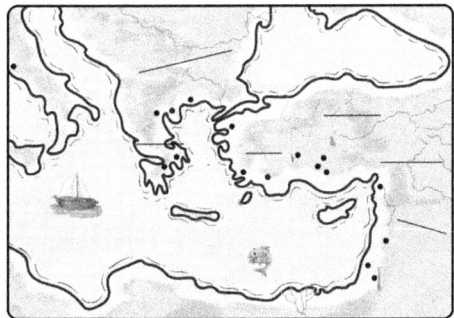

Answers in Appendix E Map 2

© Master the Bible Ministries

Old Testament 🔓

The Beginning

⁓

The Kingdom

⁓

The Prophets

CHAPTER 19

Creation and the Fall

Genesis 1-3

DIRECTIONS: Read the story to yourself. Or read it as a family with each person reading a different part aloud.

Creation

Genesis 1-2

NARRATOR: In the beginning, God created the heavens and the earth. Now the earth didn't have a shape and was empty. But the Spirit of God was hovering over the waters. And God said:

GOD: Let there be light!

NARRATOR: And there was light. God saw that the light was good. He separated the light from the darkness. God called the light "day" and the darkness he called "night." There was evening and morning—the first day.

GOD: Let there be a dome in the middle of the waters. Let it separate the waters.

NARRATOR: And that's what happened. God called the dome "sky." There was evening and morning—the second day.

GOD: Let the water under the sky be gathered into one place. And let the dry land appear.

NARRATOR: That's what happened. God called the dry ground "land." He called the waters "seas." God saw that it was good.

GOD: Let the land produce plants and trees according to their kind.

NARRATOR: Then the land produced different kinds of plants. There was evening and morning—the third day.

GOD: Let there be lights in the dome of the sky. Let them be signs to mark my festivals and days and years.

NARRATOR: So, God created the sun, moon, and stars. There was evening and morning—the fourth day.

GOD: Let the waters be filled with animals. And let birds fly above the earth.

NARRATOR: So, God created all the animals that fill the seas. There was evening and morning—the fifth day.

GOD: Let the land bring forth all kinds of living creatures.

NARRATOR: So, God made all the land animals and all the things that move on the ground. Then God said:

GOD: Let's make humans in our image and in our likeness so they can rule over the fish, the birds, and the animals on the land.

NARRATOR: God formed a person from the dust. Then God breathed into him, and the person became a living being! God placed the person he created, Adam, in a garden in the land of Eden. God brought all the wild animals to Adam to see what he would name them. But there was no creature like Adam.

GOD: It's not good for the man to be alone. I'll make a helper who is like him.

NARRATOR: From Adam's side, God made a woman and presented her to Adam.

ADAM: She is like me!

NARRATOR: God saw all that he had made, and it was very good. There was evening and morning—the sixth day. God rested on the seventh day. He blessed it and made it holy because that was the day he rested after he created everything.

God's Image

Humans are the only beings in the whole universe made in the image of God.

NARRATOR: The tree of life and the tree of the knowledge of good and evil were in the middle of the garden of Eden. God commanded Adam:

GOD: You can eat from any tree in the garden. But don't eat from the tree of the knowledge of good and evil. If you eat from it, you will certainly die.

NARRATOR: Now the serpent said to Eve:

SERPENT: You won't really die if you eat from that tree. God knows that when you eat it, you'll become like God. You'll know good and evil.

NARRATOR: When Eve saw that the fruit looked good and would make her wise, she took some and ate it. Then she gave some to her husband, who was with her, and he ate it. Their eyes were opened, and they realized they were naked. When they heard the sound of God walking in the garden, they hid from God.

GOD: Where are you?

ADAM: I heard you in the garden. I was afraid because I was naked. So I hid.

GOD: Who told you that you're naked? Did you eat from the tree I commanded you not to eat from?

ADAM: The woman you put here to be with me—she gave me some fruit from the tree, and I ate it.

Wrong Tree

Adam and Eve were completely innocent. When they ate from the wrong tree, they started judging all their actions as "good" or "evil" and felt bad about themselves if they didn't measure up. Through Jesus, God doesn't judge us. We are innocent again!

EVE: The serpent tricked me, and I ate.

NARRATOR: God said to the serpent:

GOD: Because you did this, you'll crawl on your belly! You and the woman will be enemies. Her son will attack your head. And you'll attack his heal.

NARRATOR: To the woman, God said:

GOD: I'll multiply the pain you feel when you give birth. You'll long for your husband, but he will rule over you.

NARRATOR: To the man, God said:

GOD: The ground is cursed because of what you did. With painful work, you will eat from the ground your whole life.

NARRATOR: Then God banished them from the garden. Adam named his wife Eve because she would be the mother of every living person.

Review It!

Who created everything? How did God's voice and his Spirit participate in creation?

What tree did God tell Adam and Eve not to eat from? What tree was next to it?

Who tricked Eve? What happened when Adam and Eve disobeyed?

Remember It!

SONG: *In the Beginning*

Learn these timeline events.

1. God creates everything
2. Adam and Eve sin
3. Flood
4. Tower of Babel

Think About It!

Why do you think every culture has a seven-day week? Do you rest one day a week? If you do, how do you rest?

In Genesis 1 and 2, what do people share in common with animals? How are people different from animals? What do you think it means to be made in God's image?

Why did God give Adam and Eve a choice to obey him? Why didn't God create a world where it was impossible for anything to go wrong?

I am innocent like Jesus.

Map It!

Dots show where cities are. Lines show where regions are. Label these places:

- Jerusalem/Mount Zion
- Hebron
- Bethlehem
- Lachish

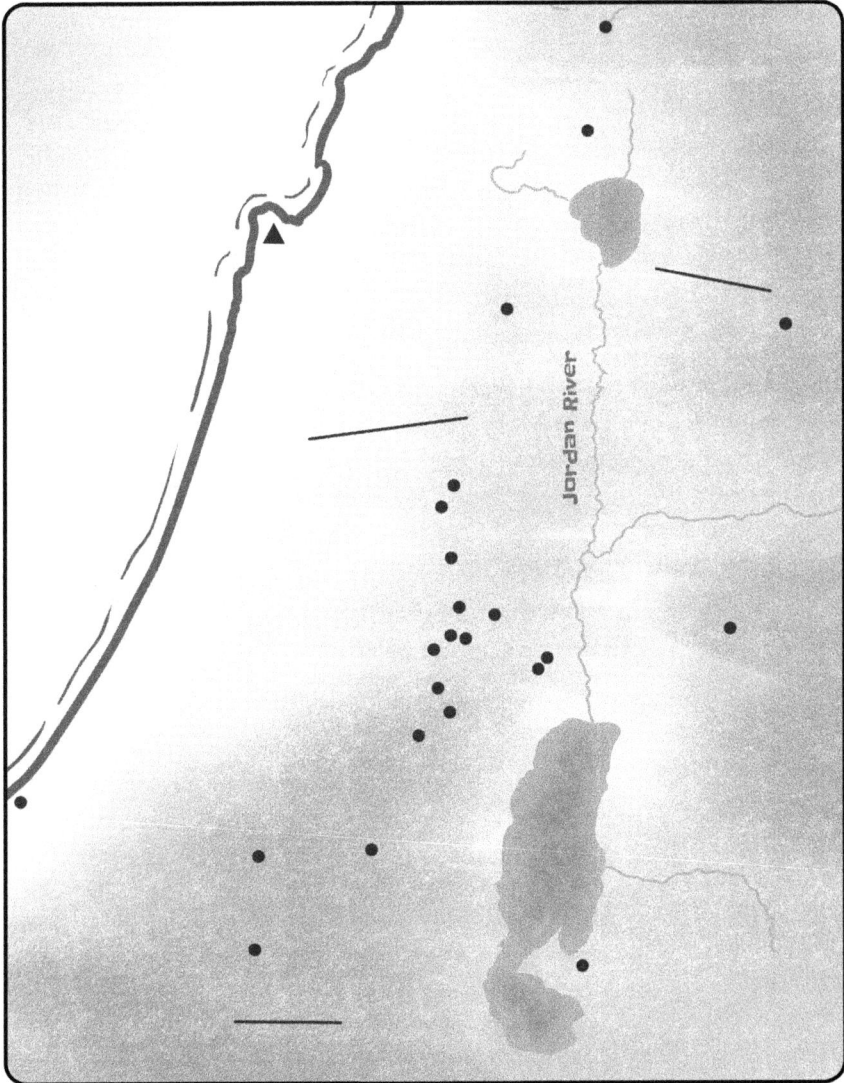

Answers in Appendix E Map 3

CHAPTER 20

The Flood and the Tower of Babel

Genesis 6-11

DIRECTIONS: Read the story to yourself. Or read it as a family with each person reading a different part aloud. When you come to a place name in **bold**, draw a tower in that location on a map in Appendix E.

The Flood

Genesis 6-9

NARRATOR: Adam and Eve had children. Some of them worshiped God. But many of them turned away from God. Before long, the human race became extremely wicked. Every thought people had was evil all the time. Plus, the sons of God had married the daughters of mortals, creating a race of people with superhuman strength. They were set on leading the earth into greater wickedness.

GOD: I will wipe humans from the earth, along with all the animals, because I regret that I made them.

NARRATOR: But Noah found favor in God's eyes. God said to him:

GOD: I'm going to end the lives of all people and animals on earth because the earth is filled with violence because of them. So, make an ark for yourself. Make it 450 feet (123 meters) long, 75 feet (23 meters) wide, and 45 feet (14 meters) high. Make three decks. I'm going to bring flood waters on the earth to destroy every creature. But I'll make a covenant with you and your sons and your wife and your sons' wives. Bring two of every creature into the ark with you, male and female, to keep them alive. Store food for the animals and for you.

NOAH: I'll do everything you said.

NARRATOR: Noah spent about 100 years building the ark. Then God told him:

GOD: Go into the ark with your family.

NARRATOR: After Noah, his family, and all the animals were safely inside the ark, God shut them in. The fountains of the deep oceans burst out. The floodgates of heaven were opened. Plus, rain fell on the earth for forty days. Noah was inside the ark with his sons—Shem, Ham, and Japheth—and their wives.

SHEM: Look! The waters are covering the highest mountains!

HAM: The water is about 23 feet (6.8 meters) above the top of the mountains!

JAPHETH: Every animal on earth has died!

NOAH'S WIFE: Praise God that he is keeping us and a pair of every animal alive!

NARRATOR: After the waters stopped filling the earth, the water slowly went down. The ark came to rest on top of a mountain. When the water had gone down enough, God said:

How Big was the Ark?

The ark was about one-and-a-half football fields long. It was taller than a four-story house. And it had the storage capacity of about 450 semi trucks.

GOD: Come out of the ark, you and all the animals.

NOAH: I'm going to build an altar to worship God.

GOD: I promise never to flood the entire earth again. The rainbow is the sign of the covenant I'm making with you. Every time I see a rainbow, I'll remember this agreement to never destroy all life again with a flood. To you and your family, I say, "Increase your numbers and fill the earth. Just as I gave you all the green plants to eat, I now give you everything to eat."

NARRATOR: From Noah's family came all the people who live in the whole earth.

NARRATOR: Sometime after the flood, the whole earth had a common language. People settled in a plain in Shinar (near **Babylon**). They said to each other:

Babel's Bad Idea

Why is building a city and skyscraper such a bad idea? From the city people wanted to rule the earth. From the tower they wanted to rule the heavens—to release evil. Confusing languages permanently stopped their plan.

PERSON 1: Let's make bricks and bake them.

PERSON 2: Let's build a city and a tower whose top is in the heavens. Then we can become important, and we won't be scattered all over the earth.

NARRATOR: God came down to see the city and the tower. He wasn't pleased.

GOD: If they work together, all speaking the same language, then nothing they plan will be impossible for them. Let's confuse their language so they won't understand each other.

NARRATOR: So, they stopped building the tower because they couldn't understand each other. Then God scattered them all over the earth. The tower they were building was called the Tower of Babel. (Babel sounds like the Hebrew word for "confused.")

Review It!

Why did God want to destroy the earth? How did God save people and animals when he punished evil?

How big was the ark Noah built?

What were people building in the plain of Shinar near Babylon?

Remember It!

SONGS: *The Flood, The Tower of Babel*

Learn these timeline events.

5. God chooses Abraham and Sarah to start a nation
6. Abraham and Sarah move to Canaan and God promises them the Land
7. Isaac, Rebecca, Jacob, Leah, Rachel—Patriarchs and Matriarchs of Israel

Think About It!

How did the flood show God's judgment of sin? How did it show his forgiveness of sin?

If you were God, would you have saved the world if only one person was righteous?

How does speaking different languages hold evil back on the earth? How does having different governments (rather than one government for the whole world) hold evil back?

I am powerful to save people like Noah.

Map It!

Dots show where cities are. Lines show where regions are. Label these places:

- Ramoth Gilead
- Beersheba
- Sodom and Gomorrah
- Jericho

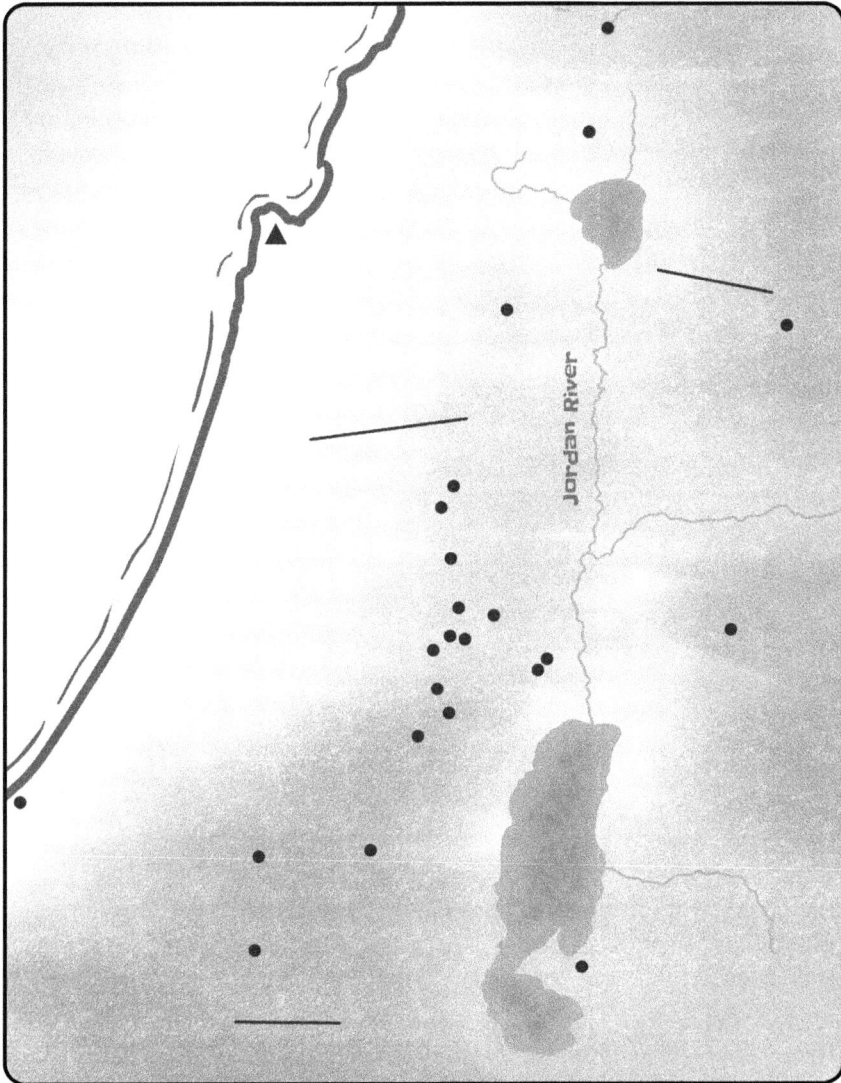

Jordan River

Answers in Appendix E Map 3

CHAPTER 21

Abraham and Sarah's Family

Genesis 11-50

DIRECTIONS: Read the story to yourself. Or read it as a family with each person reading a different part aloud. When you come to a place name in **bold**, draw a person in that location on a map in Appendix E.

Abraham and Sarah Start a Nation

Genesis 11-24

NARRATOR: After the Flood and the Tower of Babel, some people worshiped God. But many cultures started to worship idols. Why didn't God clearly show everyone his glory and tell people he is the only real God? He knew many people would reject him—even if they plainly saw who he is.

God's solution was to create a nation to show the world what he's like. Eventually, God would send a Savior through this nation. Watch as God speaks with Abraham and Sarah. They're living in the city **Ur** in **Chaldea**. Abraham is 75 years old, and Sarah is about 66.

GOD: Leave your country and your father's family. Go to the land I will show you. I'll make you into a great nation, and I will bless you. I will bless those who bless you. And whoever curses you, I will curse. All people groups on earth will be blessed through you.

ABRAHAM: I will go.

NARRATOR: When Abraham and Sarah arrived in the land of **Canaan**, God spoke to Abraham again:

GOD: I will give you and your descendants all the land that you see—from the river of **Egypt** (the **Nile**) to the **Euphrates River**.

ABRAHAM: Lord, you still haven't given me a child.

GOD: Look up at the sky. Count the stars if you can. That's how many descendants you'll have.

NARRATOR: Abraham believed God. And God credited righteous to him because he believed. But more time passed, and Abraham and Sarah still didn't have a child. So, Sarah told Abraham:

Abraham and Sarah

Why did God choose a couple that couldn't have children for a plan that required having a child? God wanted to show us that we're not saved by doing something great for God. We're saved by faith—believing what God says and following him.

SARAH: God has kept me from having children. Take my slave Hagar. Maybe you can have children through her.

NARRATOR: Hagar became pregnant and gave birth to a boy, Ishmael. Thirteen years later, God appeared to Abraham again.

GOD: I will give you a son by Sarah. You're to call him Isaac. I'll make my covenant with him.

ABRAHAM: I wish Ishmael could live before you!

GOD: I will bless Ishmael and make him a great nation. But I will make my covenant with Isaac, the son Sarah will birth next year.

NARRATOR: When Abraham was 100 and Sarah about 91, Sarah gave birth to Isaac.

SARAH: God has given me laughter. Who would have said to Abraham that I would nurse children? But God has given me a son!

NARRATOR: Abraham, Sarah, and Isaac lived near **Hebron**. When Isaac grew up, he married his cousin Rebekah.

NARRATOR: Isaac and Rebekah had twin boys, Esau and Jacob. When Rebekah was pregnant, God told her:

GOD: Two nations are inside you. One will be stronger than the other. The older will serve the younger.

NARRATOR: Esau was born first. He had all the rights of the firstborn. It looked like he would inherit God's promise to Abraham to build a nation that would show the world who God is. But Jacob wanted to have the firstborn's rights. One day Esau came in from the field starving.

Esau and Jacob

Why would God give Isaac and Rebekah twins, but only choose one to inherit Abraham's promise? To show us that anyone who seeks God will find him. We don't have to be born into a special spot.

ESAU: Feed me some of that red stew you made. I'm so hungry I could die!

JACOB: First sell me your rights as the firstborn. Swear an oath!

ESAU: Okay, I'll swear an oath.

NARRATOR: Esau didn't care about the rights that came with being born first. So, he sold them to Jacob for a bowl of stew. Later, Jacob tricked Isaac and received the blessing of the firstborn, too. Esau was furious.

ESAU: I'm going to kill Jacob as soon as our father dies.

NARRATOR: To save Jacob, Rebekah told him:

REBEKAH: Go to my brother Laban in **Paddan Aram**. Find a wife there.

NARRATOR: Jacob married two of his cousins, Leah and Rachel. He had twelve sons and grew very rich. After about twenty years, God told Jacob:

GOD: Go back to **Canaan**.

NARRATOR: Jacob and his huge family started the journey home. As they drew near to Canaan, Jacob was thinking about his brother Esau. Was Esau still mad at him? He was also thinking about the God of Abraham and Isaac. Would Jacob make God his god? Would he have a personal relationship with God, too?

JACOB: I've heard that Esau is coming to meet me with 400 men. Are they going to fight me?

NARRATOR: Just before he crossed the river to enter Canaan, Jacob wrestled with a "man" all night. As the sun was coming up, the "man" blessed him by changing his name to Israel.

JACOB: I saw God face-to-face, and I didn't die! I'm going to worship the God Abraham and Isaac worshiped. He will be my God.

NARRATOR: When Jacob met Esau, Esau hugged him. He was so glad to see Jacob again.

ESAU: God has given me everything I need. He's been generous to me.

NARRATOR: Jacob moved near **Hebron** where Isaac lived. Esau moved to **Seir**, where his descendants grew to become a great nation.

When Jacob was old, his entire family moved to **Egypt** to survive a famine. God had sent Joseph, one of Jacob's sons, to Egypt to prepare a way for them. Although Joseph started as a slave in Egypt, God promoted him to second in command. The book of Genesis ends with Jacob's family living together happily in Egypt.

Review It!

How old were Abraham and Sarah when they left Ur? How old were they when Isaac was born? How long did they have faith before they saw what they were praying for happen?

Why did Esau sell Jacob his rights as first born?

How many sons did Jacob have? What were his wives' names?

Remember It!

SONG: *Abraham*

Learn these timeline events.

8. Israel moves to Egypt and becomes slaves
9. Moses leads Israel out of slavery
10. 10 commandments and the Law

Think About It!

How was Abraham made righteous?

Why did God want to give Abraham and Sarah a son miraculously?

Why couldn't Jacob just tell God, "My father and mother worshiped you, so I must be O.K."? Why did he have to make his own decision about God?

I am a blessing to the world.

Map It!

Dots show where cities are. Lines show where regions are. Label these places:

- Ai
- Gilgal
- Gibeon
- Bethel

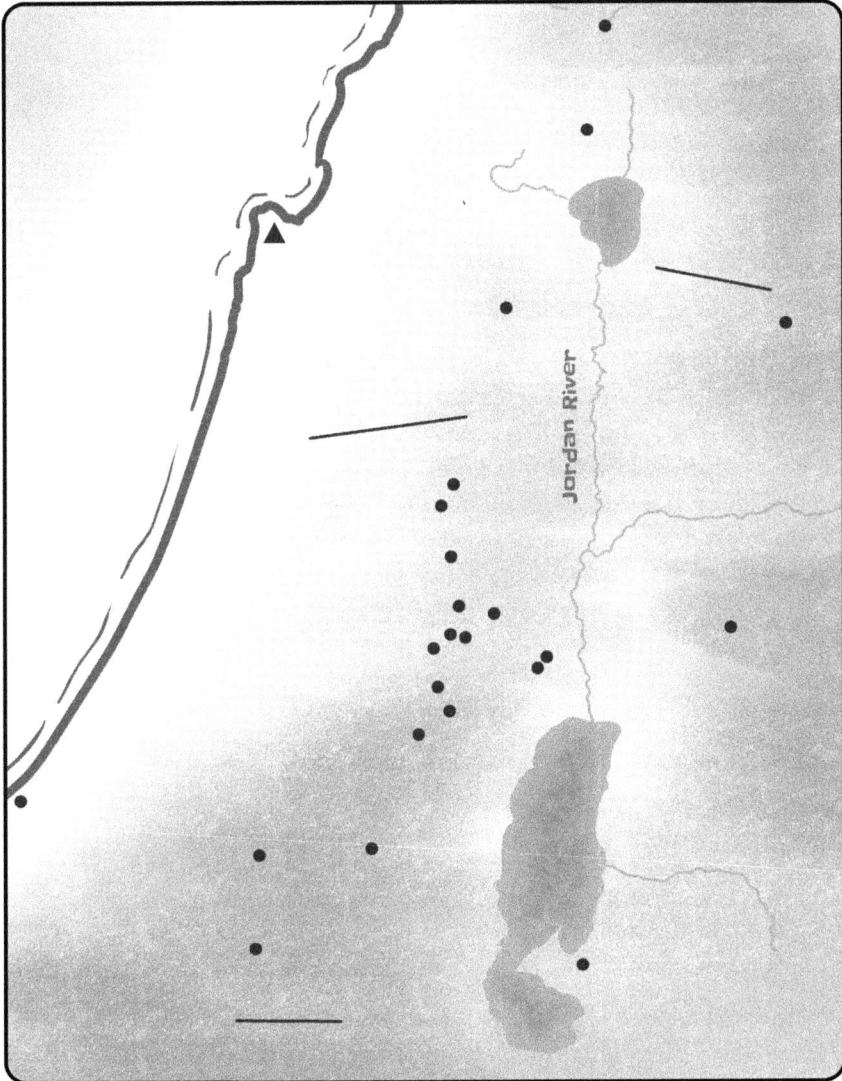

Answers in Appendix E Map 3

CHAPTER 22

Moses and the Exodus

Exodus, Leviticus, Numbers, Deuteronomy

DIRECTIONS: Read the story to yourself. Or read it as a family with each person reading a different part aloud. When you come to a place name in **bold**, draw Moses' staff in that location on a map in Appendix E.

Moses leads Israel out of Egypt
Exodus 1-15

NARRATOR: Not long after Joseph died, the Hebrew people became slaves in **Egypt**. For about 400 years they served the Egyptians. Growing fearful of the Hebrews, the king of Egypt ordered all their male babies be thrown into the **Nile River**. Bravely, a mom put her baby boy in a basket on the Nile near where a princess of Egypt liked to bathe. The baby's older sister Miriam stood nearby to watch what would happen to her brother.

PRINCESS: What is this? A little boy! He must be one of the Hebrew babies.

MIRIAM: Should I go find a Hebrew woman to nurse him for you?

PRINCESS: Yes, I will adopt him as my son. I'll call him Moses.

NARRATOR: So, Moses, born a slave, was raised as a prince of Egypt. When he grew up, God told him:

GOD: I've seen how miserable my people are. I'm going to rescue them and bring them back to Canaan. I'm sending you to tell Pharaoh to let my people go.

NARRATOR: Moses and his brother Aaron told Pharaoh:

AARON: This is what God says, "Israel is my firstborn son. Let my son go so he can worship me. If you won't let him go, I will kill your firstborn son."

NARRATOR: Pharaoh didn't listen to Moses and Aaron. At Moses' command, ten plagues were released on Egypt.

MOSES: With the staff in my hand, I'll strike the Nile. It will turn to blood.

NARRATOR: Although Pharaoh saw the sign, he wouldn't let the people go. God sent frogs, lice, flies, sickness of cattle, boils, hail, locusts, and darkness. Then God told Moses:

GOD: Each family should kill a lamb and put its blood on the door frames of the house. I will kill the firstborn son in every Egyptian house. But I will pass over the houses with the blood of the lamb on the door posts. Everyone in those houses will be safe.

PHARAOH: My firstborn son is dead! Take your people, and leave quickly!

NARRATOR: As soon as his slaves had left, Pharaoh changed his mind.

ISRAELITE: *The Egyptian army is on one side of us, and the Red Sea is on the other! We are stuck! We're going to die!*

NARRATOR: But God told Moses:

GOD: Stretch your staff over the Red Sea. I will send a wind to divide the waters so that the Israelites can walk across the sea on dry ground.

NARRATOR: All night long a strong wind blew back the sea. The entire nation crossed over with walls of water on both sides of them. When the Egyptians tried to chase them, the army was drowned.

No Way Out?

Trapped between the army and the Red Sea, the people walked through the sea. If you don't see a way out, ask God. He'll make one for you.

The Law, the Feasts, and the Tabernacle

Exodus 19-40, parts of Leviticus, Numbers, and Deuteronomy

NARRATOR: God appeared to the entire nation at **Mount Sinai**. In a thick cloud, with lightening, thunder and loud trumpet blast, God came down in fire. He spoke the words of the Ten Commandments:

GOD: I am the LORD, your God. I brought you out of slavery. Don't have any gods besides me. Don't make an idol. Don't misuse my name. Work for six days, then rest on the seventh day. I've made the seventh day holy because that's when I rested after I created everything. Honor your father and mother. Don't murder. Don't commit adultery. Don't steal. Don't give a false report that could get someone in trouble. Don't long to have something that belongs to someone else.

Hearing God

In fire and a thick cloud, God appeared on Mount Sinai. His glory nearly ripped the mountain apart. But he wanted to be there himself. God wants to be close to us. That's why God spoke the 10 Commandments himself. That's why he told Moses to build a place people could meet with him. The thing God wants more than anything is to be close to you.

NARRATOR: God gave these ten laws and many others to the nation. In the end, God wanted more than a nation who knew his ways. He wanted a people who would come very close to him. So, he told Moses to spend forty days on **Mount Sinai** with God.

MOSES: Here is the plan God gave me on the mountain. We'll build a place where we can meet with God. It will have three parts—an outer court, a Holy Place, and a Holiest Place.

[See the Tabernacle diagram in the Appendix.]

PERSON 1: What will be in the outer court?

MOSES: There will be an altar on which we'll sacrifice. Anyone who wants to give God an offering to build a friendship with him—or to ask forgiveness for doing something wrong—can bring their sacrifice there.

PERSON 2: What will be in the Holy Place?

MOSES: There will be a menorah—a candle with seven branches and seven lights. There will also be a table with fresh bread on it and an altar where priests will burn incense. The incense stands for our prayers.

PERSON 3: What will be in the Holiest Place?

MOSES: The ark—a special box—of the covenant God made with us will be there. It will be like God's throne. He'll sit above the ark.

NARRATOR: When the people finished building the Tabernacle, they poured oil on Aaron and his sons to be priests. Then the cloud of God's presence settled on the Tabernacle, and God's glory filled it.

MOSES: Every day we'll offer a morning and evening sacrifice at the Tabernacle. We'll have a special offering each Sabbath (seventh day of the week). On each new moon we'll have a bigger celebration. We'll ask God's blessing and guidance for the month. And we'll give our first and best to God each month. Then seven times a year we'll celebrate a special Festival.

PERSON 2: What are the festivals of the LORD?

MOSES: In the spring we'll have four festivals—Passover, Unleavened Bread, First Fruits, and Shavuot. In the Fall we'll have three Festivals—Trumpets, Yom Kippur, and Sukkoth.

[See Appendix D.]

PERSON 1: What do these Festivals mean?

MOSES: They are special times each year God will meet with us. They show us his plan to save us.

NARRATOR: With the laws, the Tabernacle, and his presence, God created a special nation. Israel was to be a mirror on earth of how heaven looks. The laws that made things clean pointed to a perfect place where everyone and everything was holy. The food laws pointed to a place where even our bodies were made perfect. And the sacrifices at the Tabernacle pointed to a perfect sacrifice that one day would pay humanity's debt for all sin—the sacrifice of Jesus.

Review It!

Who adopted Moses? Who were his brother and sister? How did they help him?

How many plagues did Moses perform in Egypt?

What did the people build in the desert to be a place they could meet with God? What did it look like?

How many Festivals of the LORD are there in the Bible? What are they?

Remember It!

SONG: *12 Tribes*

Learn these timeline events.

11. The Tabernacle and the Feasts
12. Joshua leads Israel into Canaan
13. 12 Judges lead Israel

Think About It!

Why did God perform signs when he brought the nation out of Egypt? Why didn't he just change Pharaoh's heart so he let them go the first time Moses asked?

How often was the Tabernacle used? What does that tell us about how often God designed us to draw near to him?

Altogether God gave Moses 613 commandments. What do the laws teach you about God's character? What do they tell you about his plans for creating a community of holy people where no disease or bad thing could enter?

I am God's dream come true.

Map It!

Dots show where cities are. Lines show where regions are. Label these places:

- Gibeah
- Ramah
- Shiloh
- Mizpah

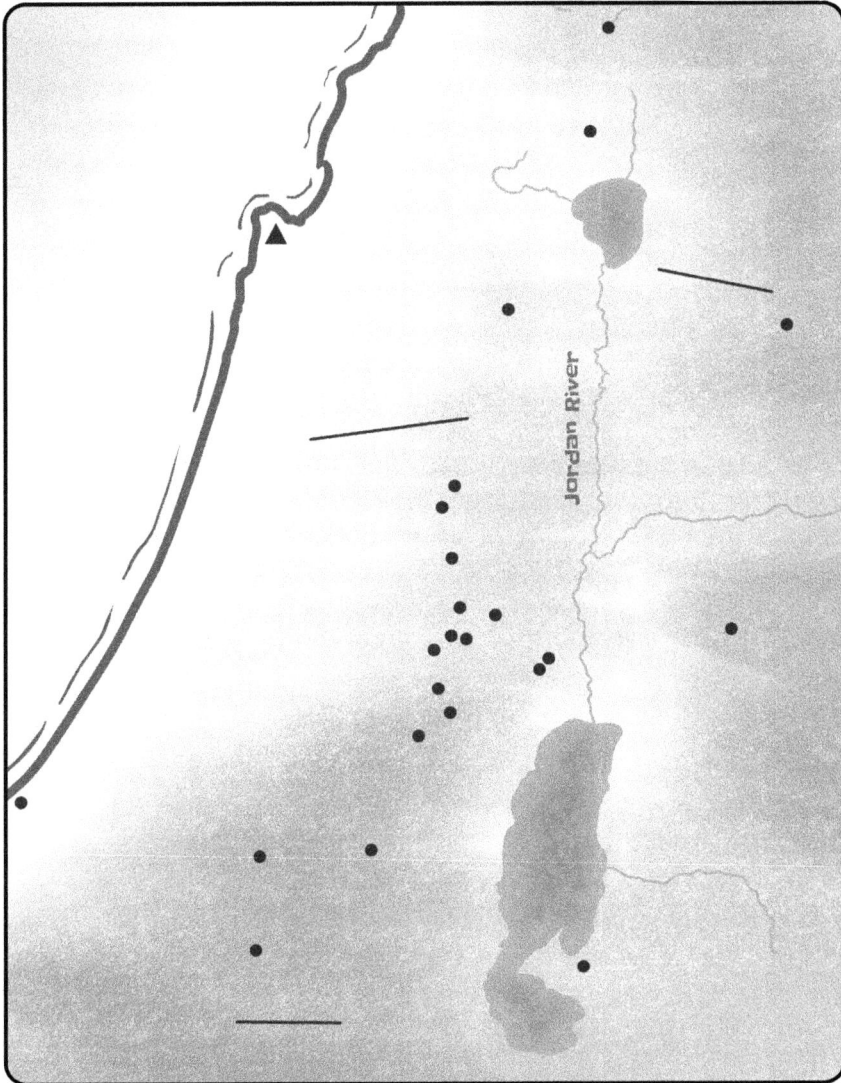

Answers in Appendix E Map 3

CHAPTER 23

Joshua and the Promise

Joshua

DIRECTIONS: Read the story to yourself. Or read it as a family with each person reading a different part aloud. When you come to a place name in **bold**, draw a sword in that location on a map in Appendix E.

Joshua takes Command
Numbers 13-14, Joshua 1, 5-6

NARRATOR: After the Israelites built the Tabernacle and after Moses wrote down all God's laws, the nation was ready to move into the land God promised to them—**Canaan**. Moses sent twelve spies, one from each tribe, into Canaan. Forty days later the spies returned with this report:

GADDI: The land is really, really good.

PALTI: But the cities are fortified and large. And we saw giants living there!

Courage

The spies thought they needed strength to enter the Promised Land. Joshua realized the thing he needed most was courage. All he had to do was try. Courage would tell him to keep going even if he felt weak.

IGAL: We seemed like grasshoppers compared to them!

JOSHUA: Let's go take the land!

CALEB: We're able to do it with God's help!

GADDI, PALTI, IGAL (AND 7 MORE SPIES): We're not able to go against these people! They're stronger than we are!

NARRATOR: Ignoring Joshua and Caleb, the people listened to the ten spies who told them they weren't strong enough to enter God's Promised Land.

ISRAELITES: We wish we had died in this wilderness! We don't want to go into the land God promised us!

NARRATOR: God gave them what they asked for. The Israelites wandered in the wilderness forty years until every adult who had decided not to enter the Promised Land died. Only Joshua and Caleb remained from that whole generation. Before Moses died, he laid his hands on Joshua to be the next leader of the nation. With God's Spirit and wisdom, Joshua would lead the Israelites into Canaan. God told Joshua:

GOD: Moses, my servant, is dead. Get ready! Cross the **Jordan River** and lead the people into the land I promised them! Be strong and brave! Do everything Moses told you to do in the law. Don't be afraid. I will be with you in everything you do.

NARRATOR: Joshua and the entire nation crossed the Jordan River. They rededicated themselves to God. Then Joshua began to prepare for his first battle. He needed to take the fortified city of **Jericho**. The logical thing to do would be to set siege to Jericho. One day Joshua saw a man standing in front of him with a drawn sword.

COMMANDER: I am the Commander of the LORD's army. You're standing on holy ground.

GOD: I'm going to defeat Jericho for you. Have all the warriors march around the city one time for six days. Have the priests march, too, carrying the ark and ram's horns. On the seventh day, march around the city seven times with the priests blowing the horns. Then give a loud battle cry. The wall around the city will collapse.

NARRATOR: Joshua had to make a decision. Would he try to take the Promised Land by doing what was logical? Or would he follow God's plan—even if it relied completely on God doing a miracle for him? Joshua chose to rely on God rather than his own strength. The wall came down just like God said! Joshua defeated Jericho in just one week!

JOSHUA: When we obey God, nothing can stop us from victory.

NARRATOR: Joshua continued to rely on God's supernatural power in every battle he fought. Five kings from cities in the south—including the kings of **Jerusalem**, **Hebron**, and **Lachish**—attacked Joshua.

JOSHUA: Sun, stand still! We need more time to defeat our enemies!

NARRATOR: God listened to Joshua. The sun stood still in the middle of the sky for about a day. It was enough time for Joshua to defeat those five kings. Then ten kings from the north attacked Joshua. But he defeated them, too. Before long, Joshua had conquered the land God promised to give Israel. Then God told him:

GOD: Joshua, divide the land among the tribes.

NARRATOR: So, Joshua gave each tribe its inheritance.

[See Map 4 in Appendix E.]

CALEB: Joshua, you know that when we spied out the land, Moses promised me an inheritance there. Give me Hebron.

JOSHUA: May God empower you to conquer Hebron!

CALEB: I know Hebron is ruled by three giants—all brothers. But if God is with me, I will conquer them. Then I'll rule the city as God promised.

NARRATOR: Caleb did defeat the three giants.

CALEB: I'm not going to stop with just defeating the giants in this city. The man who captures **Debir** can marry my daughter Acsah.

NARRATOR: Othniel, Caleb's nephew, defeated Debir. He married Acsah. Caleb gave Othniel and Acsah some land in the **Negev**. One day Acsah asked her father for a special favor.

CALEB: What would you like?

ACSAH: Please give me a special blessing. You've given me land in the Negev. Now please give me springs of water, too.

CALEB: I'll give you both the upper and lower springs.

NARRATOR: Boldness, leadership, being so close to God that we're not afraid to ask for more—Caleb, Othniel, and Acsah are examples of how God wanted his people to take the land. When Joshua was old, he told all the people to meet him at **Shechem**.

JOSHUA: This is what God says, "I gave you cities that you didn't build. I gave you vineyards and olive groves that you didn't plant. Now put aside other gods. Worship the LORD!" Choose today whom you will serve. But my family and I will worship the LORD!

ISRAELITES: The LORD saved us from slavery in Egypt. The LORD drove out the nations in this land and gave the land to us. We will worship the LORD!

Inheritance

God has an inheritance—special blessings and riches in spiritual places—for us. Caleb had three giants living in Hebron, his inheritance. Sometimes we have to move out bad things—like fear or shame—so we can have the special place God has created for us.

Review It!

Why didn't the people want to enter the land God promised them?

How did Joshua defeat Jericho?

What city did Caleb want as his inheritance? Who did he have to defeat to take it?

What did Acsah ask her dad for?

Remember It!

SONG: *First Five Books of the Bible*

Learn these timeline events.

14. Samuel anoints the first two kings, Saul and David
15. God promises David an eternal dynasty
16. David and prophetic musicians write psalms

Think About It!

From what perspective would the Israelites' decision not to enter the Promised Land seem like the best thing to do? From what perspective would it seem foolish?

What did God's plan for conquering Jericho require of Joshua? What traits did it develop in him?

How do Caleb, Othniel, and Acsah demonstrate courage, leadership, and closeness to God? Their story is the only one included in both Joshua and Judges. Why do you think it's in the Bible twice? What's so important about it?

I will succeed when I follow God's path.

Map It!

Dots show where cities are. Lines show where regions are. Label these places:

- Dan
- Jezreel
- Hazor
- Shechem
- Heshbon

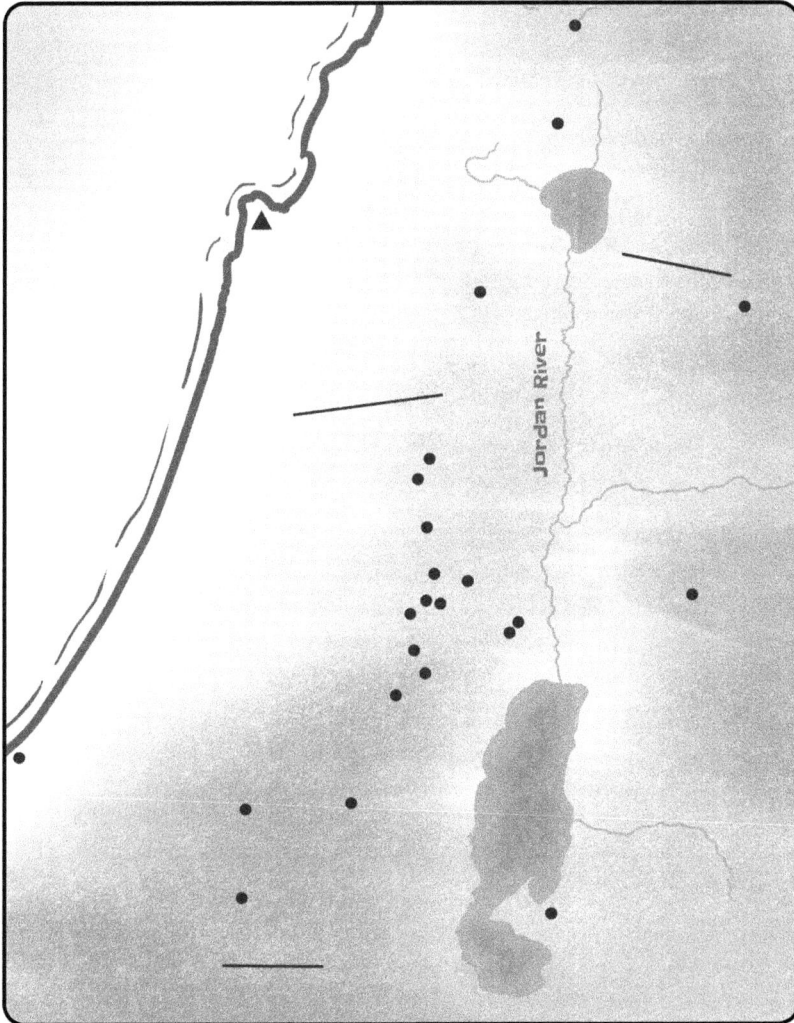

Answers in Appendix E Map 3

CHAPTER 24

Judges and Ruth

Judges and Ruth

DIRECTIONS: Read the story to yourself. Or read it as a family with each person reading a different part aloud. When you come to a place name in **bold**, draw a sheaf of wheat in that location on a map in Appendix E.

Gideon Defeats Midian | Judges 2-3, 6-8

NARRATOR: After Joshua's generation died, the Israelites forgot their promise to follow God. They began to serve the idols that the nations around them worshiped. So, God handed them over to enemies who plundered and oppressed them.

Good Enough

Gideon didn't feel good enough to do something special for God. But God knew Gideon was perfect for his special job even if he didn't feel that way—just like you are perfect for the special thing God has for you.

ISRAELITE 1: The people oppressing us are making our lives miserable!

ISRAELITE 2: We plant crops, but they steal them at harvest time. We have nothing left. Life is so difficult!

NARRATOR: When the people cried out in agony, God felt sorry for them. He'd raise up a leader—called a judge—to deliver them from the people oppressing them. The judge would turn the people back to God. There would be peace as long as that judge lived. When the judge died, people would turn away from God again. The cycle would start all over.

Twelve judges are mentioned in the book of Judges. But more is written about six of them—Othniel, Ehud, Deborah, Gideon, Jephthath, and Samson.

Altogether, Moses, Joshua, and the judges ruled Israel for about 400 years. Let's see how Gideon saved the nation. He's a good example of how God used the judges to rescue Israel.

ISRAELITE 1: **Midian** has been oppressing us for seven years! They've taken away our crops, our sheep, and our cattle! They've left us nothing to eat!

NARRATOR: One day Gideon was threshing wheat in a winepress to hide it from the Midianites.

ANGEL: The LORD is with you mighty warrior! Deliver Israel from Midian!

GIDEON: But I'm the youngest in my family. And my family is the weakest in my tribe.

NARRATOR: That night God told Gideon:

GOD: Pull down the idol in the middle of your town. Build an altar for the LORD in that spot.

NARRATOR: When the people saw that Gideon had torn down the town idol and dedicated the town to God, they were furious. They wanted to kill him. Despite their reaction, God still wanted to save them from Midian. Filled with God's Spirit, Gideon gathered an army.

GOD: Gideon, you have too many soldiers. I don't want Israel bragging that their own strength saved them. Tell any soldier who is afraid to go home.

NARRATOR: More than half of the men went home. Only 10,000 remained.

GOD: You still have too many soldiers. Bring them to some water. Put the soldiers who lap water like a dog in one group. Put those who kneel down to drink in a separate group.

NARRATOR: Only 300 men lapped water.

GOD: With those 300 men, I will deliver the entire Midianite army to you.

GIDEON: Get up, men! Take trumpets and empty jars. Position yourselves all around the Midianite camp. Watch me and do what I do. When I blow my trumpet, blow your trumpet and break your jar.

NARRATOR: When Gideon's army blew their trumpets, God caused the Midianites to attack each other and run away.

GIDEON: Cut off their retreat at the **Jordan River**! We can completely defeat them!

NARRATOR: It was a miracle. God wanted Israel to know that he loved them. Their mistakes didn't cancel God's plans for them. As soon as they turned back to God, he used his supernatural power to restore them.

Ruth Chooses God
Ruth 1-4

NARRATOR: During the time of the judges, an amazing thing happened in the town of **Bethlehem**.

ELIMELECH: There's nothing to eat in Bethlehem. Let's move to **Moab** to escape the famine.

NARRATOR: Elimelech, his wife Naomi, and their two sons moved to Moab. The boys married Moabite women. Then all the men died.

NAOMI: Life has been bitter for me. I'm moving back to Bethlehem because I've heard there are abundant crops there now.

NARRATOR: Naomi told her two daughters-in-law to remain in Moab to remarry. One of them did, but Ruth refused. She told Naomi:

RUTH: Wherever you go, I will go. Wherever you live, I will live. Your people will be my people. Your God will be my God.

NARRATOR: So, Ruth left the idols of Moab, and clung to Israel's God for help. The two women returned to Bethlehem at the beginning of the grain harvest.

More

Even though her situation seemed hopeless, Ruth trusted in God. When he gave her a baby, she was so happy! God provided for her way beyond what she expected. God loves to give us more than we ask for.

RUTH: Let me go gather grain in the fields so that we can have something to eat.

NARRATOR: Ruth just happened to be working in the fields of Boaz, one of Elimelech's relatives. When Boaz noticed her, he told Ruth:

BOAZ: May the LORD reward your efforts! You've come to the LORD to protect you. May he repay your kindness to Naomi.

NARRATOR: At the end of the harvest season, Boaz and Ruth married. God enabled Ruth to have a baby.

VILLAGE WOMAN: God has blessed you, Naomi! May this child become famous in Israel! Your daughter-in-law, who loves you, is better to you than seven sons!

NARRATOR: They named the baby Obed. He was the father of Jesse, who was David's father. So, Ruth, from Moab, became the great-grandmother of Israel's King David—and an ancestor to Jesus! Ruth's trust in God did provide for her. But it also birthed something that blessed the whole world—a dynasty founded on trust in God.

Review It!

Why was Midian oppressing Israel? What had Israel done wrong?

How many men were in Gideon's army? Was it enough to defeat Midian?

What were the bad things that happened to Ruth? What were the good things that happened to her?

Who was the baby that God supernaturally enabled Ruth to have? Why were Ruth and her baby important?

Remember It!

SONG: *Joshua to Samuel*

Learn these timeline events.

17. Solomon builds the Temple
18. Solomon writes wise books
19. Israel divides into two kingdoms—Israel and Judah

Think About It!

Why do you think God told Gideon to pull down the idol in the middle of the town and to build an altar to the LORD there? What did that have to do with defeating Midian? What principle does it show us for our lives?

Why did God want Israel to know that the victory over Midian was from God?

Ruth went through a lot of hard things. Her husband died. She became poor. What would Ruth's life had been like if none of those bad things had happened? Do you think she would have left Moab and become an ancestor of David and Jesus? How can difficult things be a doorway into a better path?

God thinks I'm good enough even when I don't.

Map It!

Dots show where cities are. Lines show where regions are. Label these places:

- Jordan River
- Salt Sea (Dead Sea)
- Great Sea (Mediterranean Sea)

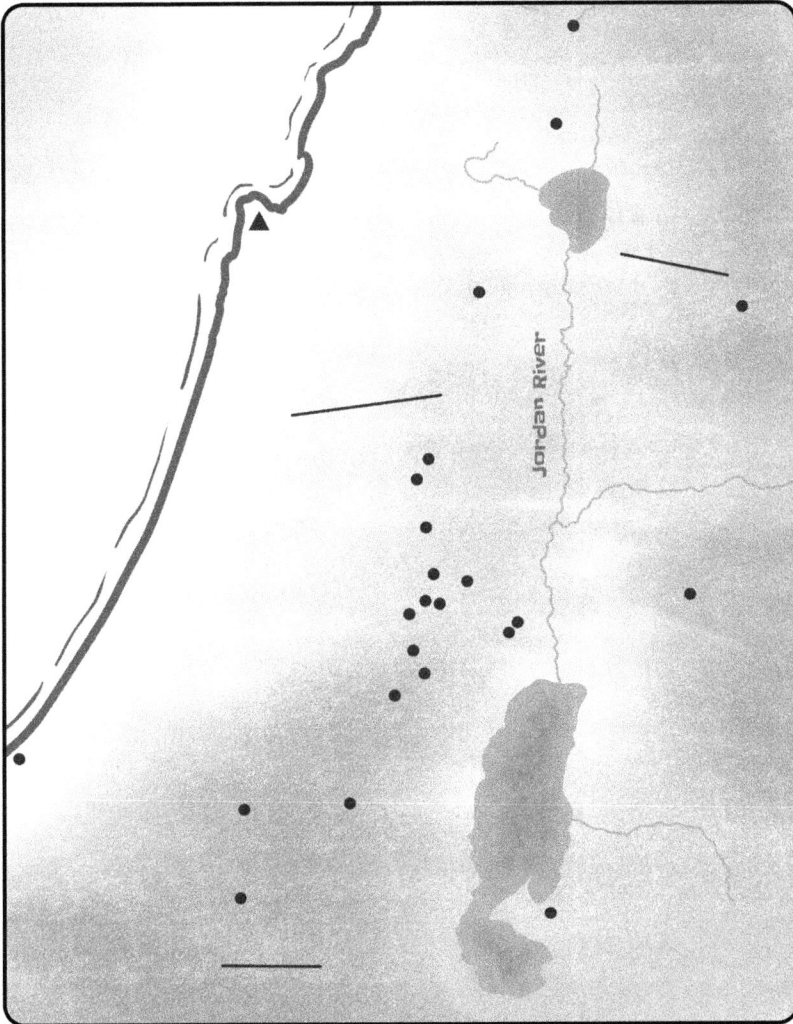

Jordan River

Answers in Appendix E Map 3

CHAPTER 25

The Kingdom Begins

1-2 Samuel, 1 Kings, 1 Chronicles

DIRECTIONS: Read the story to yourself. Or read it as a family with each person reading a different part aloud. When you come to a place name in **bold**, draw a crown in that location on a map in Appendix E.

Saul and David

1 Samuel 8-17, 2 Samuel 7

NARRATOR: At the end of the time of the judges, God raised up Israel's last judge—and first prophet. His name was Samuel. God spoke to Samuel all the time with messages for the nation. When he grew old, the people came to Samuel at **Ramah**.

ISRAELITES: Appoint a king to rule over us like all the other nations!

NARRATOR: Although Samuel was troubled by the request, God told him:

GOD: Do what the people are asking.

NARRATOR: God directed Samuel to anoint Saul from **Gibeah** as king. He was a tall, handsome man. Early in his kingship, God tested Saul.

SAMUEL: You're gathering an army to fight the **Philistines**. Wait for me seven days. I'll come and make offerings to God. Then you can attack.

NARRATOR: Saul waited seven days for Samuel. Each day, the Philistines gathered more troops. Each day more Israelite soldiers snuck away from Saul's army. Afraid that he'd lose the battle if he waited any longer, Saul said:

SAUL: Bring me the burnt offering and peace offerings. I'll offer them myself.

NARRATOR: As soon as Saul offered the sacrifices, Samuel arrived.

SAMUEL: You've been foolish! You offered the sacrifices yourself when God told you to wait for me. If you had obeyed God, he would have given you a dynasty over Israel forever. Now God will look for a man who is loyal to him to rule Israel!

God First

God doesn't look at us from the outside. He doesn't care about how many good things we do that impress people. He looks inside us. When we put God first, he moves us ahead of everyone else to a place of honor.

NARRATOR: Saul remained king until he died many years later. But Saul lost his ability to start a dynasty, where his son and grandson would rule after him. God began looking for someone who wanted God more than anything else. He would make that person the next king.

GOD: Samuel, go to **Bethlehem**. There I've chosen a king for myself.

NARRATOR: Samuel anointed the youngest son of Jesse, Ruth's grandson, to become king when he grew up. His name was David. The Spirit of God came on David powerfully. David even volunteered to fight a giant from Philistia named Goliath. He was threatening Israel.

DAVID: You're coming against me with a lot of weapons. But I'm coming against you in the name of the LORD, Israel's God! He will give you into my hands! Then everyone will know that God doesn't need weapons to defeat his enemies.

NARRATOR: David did defeat Goliath with a slingshot. Then David became a general in Saul's army and married Saul's daughter. Eventually, Saul realized God had chosen David as the next king. Saul tried to kill him. After years of running from Saul and deepening his trust in God, David became king!

DAVID: God has made me king in **Jerusalem**! He's given me riches and victory in my battles! I'm living in a palace. But God's house is a tent. I want to build him a great temple.

NARRATOR: Nathan, one of the king's prophets, told David:

NATHAN: God says, "Your son will build a temple for me. And God himself will build a dynasty for you. You will be famous, and your dynasty will last forever."

NARRATOR: Through disobedience, Saul lost the chance to build a permanent dynasty. But David's trust in God created an everlasting kingdom. Through his dynasty, the world's Savior, Jesus, would come.

Solomon
1 Chronicles 22, 1 Kings 3, 6-11

DAVID: Solomon, my son, God has chosen you to build a temple for him. May God give you insight and understanding so that you will have success as a king!

NARRATOR: When David died, Solomon became the next king. He used to offer a thousand burnt offerings to God. One night after Solomon offered many sacrifices, God appeared to him in a dream at **Gibeon**.

GOD: Ask me for anything you want me to give you.

SOLOMON: You've made me king although I'm young and inexperienced. Give me wisdom so I can make wise decisions for your people.

GOD: You could have asked me for long life, or riches, or victory over your enemies. But you asked me for wisdom. I will give you a wise mind greater than anyone before or after you. I'll also give you riches and honor so you'll be the greatest king of your time.

Love

Solomon was very wise. But he left God when he loved people who worshiped other gods. Loving God will keep us connected to him more than wisdom— or anything else.

NARRATOR: Solomon became very wise—and wealthy and famous. He built a huge palace for himself. He had enormous amounts of gold and silver. In fact, silver wasn't even considered valuable in Solomon's kingdom because there was so much of it. He was wealthier and wiser than all the kings of the earth. But the greatest thing Solomon did was build a temple for God. When the temple was finished, Solomon gathered the nation in **Jerusalem**.

SOLOMON: I certainly built an exalted temple where you can live, God! Watch over this temple night and day. When people pray to you in this temple, listen from heaven and answer their prayers.

NARRATOR: The cloud of the LORD's glory filled the temple.

PRIEST: We can't do our jobs at the temple today because of the cloud. God's glory is filling the temple!

NARRATOR: When Solomon grew older, the foreign wives he married turned his heart from God to their idols. The prophet Ahijah spoke to Jeroboam, a young, talented leader of Solomon's work crews:

PROPHET AHIJAH: Here's what God says, "Because Solomon abandoned me, I will tear the kingdom away from his son. I'll give you ten pieces of it, Jeroboam."

NARRATOR: Solomon became the greatest king of his time because he asked God for what he needed to help other people. Riches or fame or a long life would have helped him. But wisdom would help the people in his kingdom. By putting others first, Solomon became great. When he turned away from God, God didn't abandon him. But he did discipline Solomon by promising to tear most of the kingdom away from his son.

Review It!

Who anointed Saul and David to be king?

Why didn't Saul's son become king after him? Why did God pick David?

What did Solomon ask God to give him?

Pretend you lived in Solomon's kingdom. How much gold and silver did you have? What did you see Solomon building?

Remember It!

SONG: *Six Main Judges, verse 1*
Honors! Add verse 2

Learn these timeline events.

> 20. Jeroboam sets up idols in Israel
> 21. Asa's reforms in Judah
> 22. Ahab marries Jezebel who establishes Baal worship in Israel

Think About It!

What did Saul lose through his disobedience? What did he not lose?

Why was it important that Solomon built a temple for God to replace the Tabernacle Moses built?

Why do you think the Bible mentions that Solomon had offered a thousand burnt offerings before God appeared to him? Was God's offer to give Solomon anything he wanted related to Solomon's sacrifice to God?

God loves it when I put him first.

Map It!

Label these tribes:

- Reuben
- Simeon
- Judah
- Gad

Answers in Appendix E Map 4

CHAPTER 26

The Kingdom Divides

1 Kings, 2 Chronicles

DIRECTIONS: Read the story to yourself. Or read it as a family with each person reading a different part aloud. When you come to a place name in **bold**, draw a crown in that location on a map in Appendix E.

Kings Rehoboam and Jeroboam

1 Kings 12, 14, 2 Chronicles 10

NARRATOR: When Solomon died, the nation gathered at **Shechem** to make his son Rehoboam king.

ISRAELITES: Your father forced us to work hard to build things for his kingdom. If you make our workload less, then we'll serve you.

REHOBOAM: Come back in three days, and I'll give you my answer.

NARRATOR: Rehoboam asked his advisors what he should do. The older advisors who had served Solomon said:

No Takebacks

Jeroboam knew he wasn't as rich or wise as Solomon. He was afraid the people wouldn't want to keep him as king. He forgot that he was exactly the person God wanted to lead. What God gives us, God won't take away.

OLDER ADVISOR: Do what the people ask, and they'll be your servants.

NARRATOR: Rejecting this advice, Rehoboam asked the younger advisors. They said:

YOUNGER ADVISOR: Tell them, "I'm much harsher than my father. I'll make it worse for you."

NARRATOR: Foolishly, Rehoboam followed their advice. When the people heard Rehoboam's response, they shouted:

ISRAELITES: We won't make you our king! Let's go home!

NARRATOR: Only the cities in Judah followed Rehoboam. The northern tribes made Jeroboam king, Although God had chosen Jeroboam, he became afraid. He thought that if the people worshiped in **Jerusalem**, they would return to King Rehoboam. After asking his advisors what he should do, Jeroboam announced:

JEROBOAM: Don't go to Jerusalem to worship God. Look, I made golden statues that look like calves. I'll put one in **Bethel** and one in **Dan**. Go there to worship!

NARRATOR: Jeroboam set up a system that looked similar to the one God gave Moses. It had major holidays at the same time as the Bible holidays. Many of the traditions were the same. But they weren't following God's words.

PROPHET AHIJAH: God says, "I tore the kingdom away from David's family line to give it to you, Jeroboam. But you've turned away from me by making gods out of metal. I'll burn up your royal house."

NARRATOR: For 200 years, God anointed many new kings, hoping they would turn the nation back to God. But no king ever removed the idols in Bethel and Dan. These idols were a main reason the northern kingdom was removed from their land later.

King Asa, King Ahab, and Prophet Elijah   1 Kings 15-18

NARRATOR: David's family line ruled the kingdom now called Judah. Some of the kings followed God. Others didn't.

KING ASA OF JUDAH: I want the nation to return to worshiping the LORD like David did. I'll remove all the idols and gross practices my ancestors set up.

NARRATOR: God blessed Asa's reign. He ruled for 41 years. In Israel, the northern kingdom, Jeroboam's family line was destroyed. King Omri built a new capital in **Samaria**. His son Ahab became the next king.

KING AHAB OF ISRAEL: I'm going to marry Jezebel, a princess from the powerful nation Sidon.

NARRATOR: When Jezebel became queen, she started a new policy.

QUEEN JEZEBEL OF ISRAEL: In **Sidon**, we worship a god called Baal. I'm going to make everyone in Israel worship Baal. I'm going to use the money people pay in taxes to build a temple for Baal and hire priests for Baal. I'm going to ask all the LORD's prophets to prophesy in Baal's name. If they refuse to worship Baal, I'll kill them.

NARRATOR: God was angered that the king and queen were trying to stop everyone from worshiping him. He sent his prophet Elijah to announce:

PROPHET ELIJAH: There will be no rain until I say so.

NARRATOR: God was giving the nation a crisis that Baal couldn't solve. He wanted people to turn back to him. Three years went by with no rain. Ahab and Jezebel continued to mistreat people who worshiped the LORD. God wanted to end the drought. So, he sent Elijah to Ahab again.

Wise or Foolish?

Sometimes what seems wise can actually be very foolish. Ahab thought it was smart to marry a princess from a powerful nation. But from God's perspective, it's foolish to become close to people who hate him. They will pull us into disaster.

PROPHET ELIJAH: Tell everyone to meet me at **Mount Carmel**. Make sure the 850 prophets that Jezebel supports are there, too.

NARRATOR: With the nation gathered at Mount Carmel, Elijah asked:

PROPHET ELIJAH: How long will it take you to decide who to worship? If the LORD is the true God, follow him! If it's Baal, follow him! Let Baal's prophets take a bull and place it on the altar. I'll do the same with another bull. Then Baal's prophets will ask their god to set the sacrifice on fire. I'll ask the LORD. Whoever responds with fire is the true God.

NARRATOR: All day long, Baal's prophets yelled and jumped around. Nothing happened. At noon Elijah made fun of them:

PROPHET ELIJAH: Try yelling louder! Maybe your god is taking a trip. Or maybe he's asleep and you need to wake him up.

NARRATOR: Then Elijah built a stone altar, put the bull on top, and poured twelve jars of water over it. At the time of the evening sacrifice, Elijah prayed.

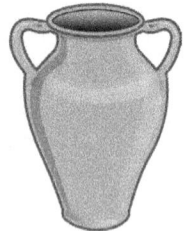

PROPHET ELIJAH: Answer me, O LORD, so these people will know that you are the true God and that you are turning their hearts back to you.

NARRATOR: Fire from the LORD fell from the sky. It burned up the offering, the wood, the stone, the dirt, and the water.

Israelites: The LORD is the true God! The LORD is the true God!

NARRATOR: When the people got rid of Baal's prophets, Elijah prayed for rain. Then rain poured down. The drought was over!

Review It!

Whose advice did Rehoboam follow? Was it good advice? Who became king of the northern kingdom called Israel? Where did he set up places to worship?

Why wasn't there enough rain? What challenge did Elijah announce to see who the true God is?

Remember It!

KEY PEOPLE SONG: *Kings of Israel—Joash to Hoshea*

MAP SONG: *Tribes of Israel*

TIMELINE SONG:

Learn these timeline events.

23. Elijah confronts Baal's prophets on Mount Carmel
24. Jehoshaphat honors God but makes a bad alliance
25. Elijah and Elisha run schools to train prophets

Think about It!

Why did Jeroboam think it was a good idea to set up idols? Why didn't he realize that God wouldn't be happy with his plan?

Why would it have seemed wise for Ahab to marry Jezebel from an earth-centered point of view? Why would it be foolish from God's point of view?

Why do you think people didn't immediately turn to God when they didn't have enough rain? Why did it take three years and a showdown between Elijah and Baal's prophets?

God made me like Elijah. He gave me an ability to listen to him and talk to him in prayer.

Label these tribes:

- Naphtali
- Gad
- Ashur
- Issachar

Answers in Appendix E Map 4

CHAPTER 27

The Kingdom Rescued

2 Kings, 2 Chronicles

DIRECTIONS: Read the story to yourself. Or read it as a family with each person reading a different part aloud. When you come to a place name in **bold**, draw a flask of oil in that location on a map in Appendix E.

Jehu Destroys Baal   2 Kings 9-10

NARRATOR: Elijah trained a prophet to replace him. His name was Elisha. Together they led communities in **Bethel** and **Jericho** that trained hundreds of prophets for the LORD. When Ahab's son Joram was king, Elisha told a young prophet he was training:

ELISHA: Go to the army in **Ramoth Gilead**. Anoint Jehu to be the next king.

NARRATOR: Jehu was an army officer who hated Baal worship. He was Israel's best hope for removing idols and turning back to the LORD.

JEHU: King Joram is at **Jezreel**. I'll drive my chariot there.

Cleaning Up

God knew the first thing Jehu would do as king is throw out Baal worship. God loves it when we clean out things that are competing with him for our attention.

JORAM: Is everything okay, Jehu?

JEHU: How can everything be okay when your mother Jezebel promotes idol worship?

NARRATOR: Jehu removed Joram from being king. He removed Jezebel from being queen mother. Then he set a trap for Baal's prophets.

JEHU: I'm going to worship Baal much more than Ahab did. Tell all of Baal's prophets to come to **Samaria** for a great sacrifice.

Make sure all of them are there!

NARRATOR: But Jehu was tricking them. When all of Baal's prophets entered the temple for Baal, Jehu commanded:

JEHU: Make sure none of the LORD's servants are inside. Now get rid of all of Baal's prophets. Then tear down the temple!

NARRATOR: So, Jehu eliminated Baal worship in Israel. (But he didn't remove the idols in **Bethel** and **Dan**.) God was so pleased that Jehu had removed Baal worship that God told him:

GOD: You've done well. Your family will rule Israel for four generations.

Athaliah Almost Destroys Judah | 2 Kings 11-12; 2 Chronicles 22-23

NARRATOR: Meanwhile in the southern kingdom, Judah had been ruled by good King Jehoshaphat. Like Asa, he turned Judah back to God. But he made a huge mistake. He married his son to Athaliah—a princess from Ahab's family. She brought up her son to worship idols like Ahab's family did. Athaliah's son became king of Judah. He was visiting his cousin, King Joram of Israel, when Jehu arrived. When Jehu killed Joram, he also killed Judah's king!

Selfish

QUEEN ATHALIAH: My son is dead. Now I will make myself queen of Judah! I'll destroy all of David's descendants! I'll be the only ruler!

NARRATOR: But one princess saw what Athaliah was doing. Acting boldly, Princess Jehosheba hid her nephew Joash from Athaliah.

Leaders are supposed to think about what's best for the people they're leading—not what's best for them. Athaliah did what she wanted to do. But Jehoida did what was best for the people. He made someone else king. God honors us when we think of others first.

PRINCESS JEHOSHEBA: Joash, you are just a baby now. But one day you'll be king. I'll hide you in the temple of the LORD here in **Jerusalem**. My husband Jehoiada is a priest. We'll keep you safe and raise you.

NARRATOR: After seven years of hiding Joash, Jehoiada decided to act.

He realized it was time to make Joash king. Summoning army officers and the royal bodyguard, he showed them the king's son.

PRIEST JEHOIADA: Here's the plan: Two units will protect the king. The rest will guard the palace. Don't let anyone come close to the king!

NARRATOR: Jehoiada led Joash to the front of the temple. He placed the crown on his head.

CROWD: Long live the king!

NARRATOR: Athaliah heard the noise. Running to the temple, she yelled:

QUEEN ATHALIAH: Treason!

PRIEST JEHOIADA: Grab her!

NARRATOR: Athaliah's rule of Judah ended. Seven-year-old Joash became king. He ruled forty years. Following Jehoiada's guidance, Joash turned the people back to God. Joash removed the temple of Baal in Jerusalem. He repaired the LORD's temple. The nation was saved!

Review It!

Who did Elisha tell the prophet to anoint as the next king?

How did Jehu trick the priests of Baal?

What was Athaliah's plan?

How did princess Jehosheba save the kingdom

Remember It!

SONG: *Kings of Israel, Joash-Hoshea*

Honors! Add What did the Kings Do? verses 3-4

Learn these timeline events.

    26. Jehu removes Baal from Israel

    27. Joash overthrows Athaliah's rule in Judah

    28. Uzziah conquers and becomes proud

Think About It!

Since Jehu rid Israel of Baal worship, why do you think he didn't throw out the idols in Bethel and Dan? How do you think God felt about keeping those idols?

Why did it matter if Athaliah or Joash ruled Judah?

Thinking about the prophetic school Elijah and Elisha led, how many people were trained to listen to God in the Old Testament? If they could listen to God, is it possible for you to hear God's direction, too?

God loves when I am friends with people who honor God.

Label these tribes:

- Zebulun
- Ephraim
- Manasseh
- Benjamin

Answers in Appendix E Map 4

© Master the Bible Ministries

CHAPTER 28

The Kingdom Falls

2 Kings, 2 Chronicles

DIRECTIONS: Read the story to yourself. Or read it as a family with each person reading a different part aloud. When you come to a place name in **bold**, draw an "X" in that location on a map in Appendix E.

Israel Falls

2 Kings 14, 17; Amos 3, 7; Hosea 1, 3, 6:1-2

NARRATOR: Jehu's great-grandson Jeroboam became king of Israel. He regained control of **Damascus** and **Hamath**, fulfilling what the prophet Jonah had said:

PROPHET JONAH: Jeroboam will expand the territory of Israel.

NARRATOR: But Jeroboam forgot about the LORD. He worshiped the idols at **Bethel** and **Dan**. For about 200 years, God had urged Israel's leaders to remove the idols. God decided to give them one last chance. He sent a prophet named Amos from **Judah** to Bethel.

PROPHET AMOS: God says, "People are taking advantage of the poor! People are worshiping idols in Bethel! Because of these sins, I will remove Israel from the land if people don't change what they're doing. These altars in Bethel will be destroyed!"

NARRATOR: God raised up another prophet named Hosea from Israel with the same message.

PROPHET HOSEA: God says, "I will punish Jehu's dynasty. Because you have chased after idols, I will send you into exile. But later I will buy you back. I'll pay a huge price to have you be my wife again."

NARRATOR: Jeroboam was so rich and successful that he didn't listen to God's warnings. The nation didn't think they needed to change. When Jeroboam died, Israel had six kings in about 20 years. Finally, the last king, Hoshea, came to the throne.

KING HOSHEA: Assyria is now a great kingdom, conquering the world. I agreed to pay Assyria's king money. But I'm going to break my treaty. I'll join with **Egypt's** king to fight against Assyria.

NARRATOR: When Hoshea broke his promise to Assyria, it was the limit of God's patience. That sin, added to all the sins of the previous kings, triggered God's punishment. Assyria captured **Samaria** and sent the people away from their land. God had made Israel a nation so that they could show the world who the true God is. How could Israel reveal God if they weren't worshiping God themselves?

PROPHET HOSEA: Let's return to the LORD. He's torn us to pieces, but he'll heal us! After two days he will revive us. On the third day, he will raise us up. Then we'll live in his presence.

Discipline

Being disciplined is good. It means your parents love you and believe you can accomplish God's purpose for your life. In the end, discipline will remove things that will hold you back. It will empower the good things to grow.

Judah Falls   2 Kings 18-19, 21-22, 25; Zephaniah 1; Jeremiah 21, 25, 29, 38, 52

NARRATOR: When Israel fell, Joash's descendant Hezekiah was king of **Judah**. **Assyria** attacked Judah, too. But Hezekiah obeyed God with his whole heart. Fervently, he asked God to save Judah. The prophet Isaiah told him:

PROPHET ISAIAH: The king of Assyria won't even shoot an arrow at **Jerusalem**. He'll go back the way he came.

NARRATOR: During the night the LORD's angel killed 185,000 Assyrian soldiers. So, the king of Assyria took down the army tents and went home. Hezekiah's obedience to the LORD saved the nation! Although Hezekiah followed God with his whole heart, his son Manasseh was the worst king in Judah's history.

KING MANASSEH: I'll set up the altars for Baal that my father tore down. I'll build altars to the stars in the LORD's temple. I'll set up a pit for magicians to speak to evil spirits. If anyone opposes me, I'll kill them.

UNKNOWN PROPHET: You've done more evil than the nations who were living here before God gave Israel this land! You've stained Jerusalem with the blood of innocent people! God will destroy Jerusalem just like Samaria! God will wipe Jerusalem clean.

NARRATOR: The Assyrians exiled Manasseh to **Babylon**. Then Manasseh humbled himself. God made him king again.

KING MANASSEH: I'm going to remove all the foreign gods. I'll clean out the LORD's temple. Judah, serve only the LORD, the God of Israel!

NARRATOR: Manasseh's grandson Josiah was the last good king. When his officials restored the LORD's temple, they made an amazing discovery:

SCRIBE SHAPHAN: We found a book! It's the law of God!

NARRATOR: Finding the Bible helped turn the nation back to God. So did prophets like Zephaniah and Jeremiah.

PROPHET ZEPHANIAH: God says, "I'm going to attack Judah and Jerusalem! I'm going to remove Baal worship! The day of the LORD's anger will burn up evil!"

NARRATOR: When Josiah heard God's law and God's plan to bring judgment, he humbled himself. So, God made him a promise. Through the prophetess Huldah, God declared:

PROPHETESS HULDAH: "I am going to bring disaster on this place because people will abandon me to worship other gods. But I won't do it in Josiah's time. He humbled himself before me."

NARRATOR: As long as Josiah was king, Judah prospered. But the kings after Josiah clung to idols. The prophet Jeremiah warned:

PROPHET JEREMIAH: If you don't repent, God will send the Babylonians against Jerusalem. They will destroy the LORD's temple. They'll carry the people into exile.

NARRATOR: Just as Jeremiah prophesied, the Babylonians surrounded Jerusalem. Zedekiah, the last king, had to make a choice. Desperate, he asked Jeremiah for advice.

KING ZEDEKIAH: The Babylonians have set siege to the city. What should I do?

PROPHET JEREMIAH: Surrender. God wants the Babylonians to capture the city because the people have turned away from God. If you surrender to them, the city won't be burned. Your family will be spared.

But if you don't surrender, the Babylonians will burn the city down and capture your family.

KING ZEDEKIAH: I'm too afraid to trust that God will protect me.

NARRATOR: Zedekiah didn't surrender. On the Ninth of Av (the fourth month), Babylonian soldiers broke through the walls of Jerusalem, burned the city, and destroyed the temple. They carried the people into exile in Babylon. God had showed Jeremiah what would happen in advance. God also showed him how long the exile would last.

PROPHET JEREMIAH: God says, "At the end of seventy years, I'll remember Israel again. I'll punish Babylon, and I'll return you to your homeland."

NARRATOR: Israel and Judah were exiled because they stopped worshiping the LORD only. But God never intended their exile to be permanent. As a loving father, he was disciplining his children to restore their purpose. He created Israel to show the world who the LORD is. Although they had forgotten him for a short time, they would return to him. Like a light to the world, they would shine again—lighting up God for everyone to see.

Humility

When Josiah was told what he was doing wrong, he didn't deny it. He wasn't mad at the person telling him. He was sorry, and he changed. When we react with humility, God honors us.

Review It!

Which prophets did God send to warn Jeroboam to repent? Did he listen?

Who was the last king of Israel? Which country defeated him?

Which kings of Judah were in today's lesson? Which ones were good? Which ones were bad?

Which prophets warned the kings of Judah? Did they listen?

Remember It!

SONG: *Kings of Judah, Saul-Azariah*
Honors! Add What did the Kings Do? verses 5-6

Learn these timeline events.

29. Jeroboam II extends Israel's territory but doesn't turn to God

30. Jonah and Amos prophesy in Israel

31. Israel falls to Assyria and is exiled

32. Hosea, Isaiah, and Micah prophesy

Think About It!

Explain in your own words why Israel and Judah went into exile. What was bad about the exile? What was good about it?

What do you think would have happened if Zedekiah had surrendered to Babylon? Do you think God usually has a way to make discipline from him less difficult?

Compare Jeroboam and Josiah. How were the prophecies they received similar? How was their reaction different?

God doesn't remember my sins anymore
when I ask him to forgive me.

Dots show where cities are. Lines show where regions are. Label these places:

- Samaria
- Gilead
- Negev
- Mount Carmel

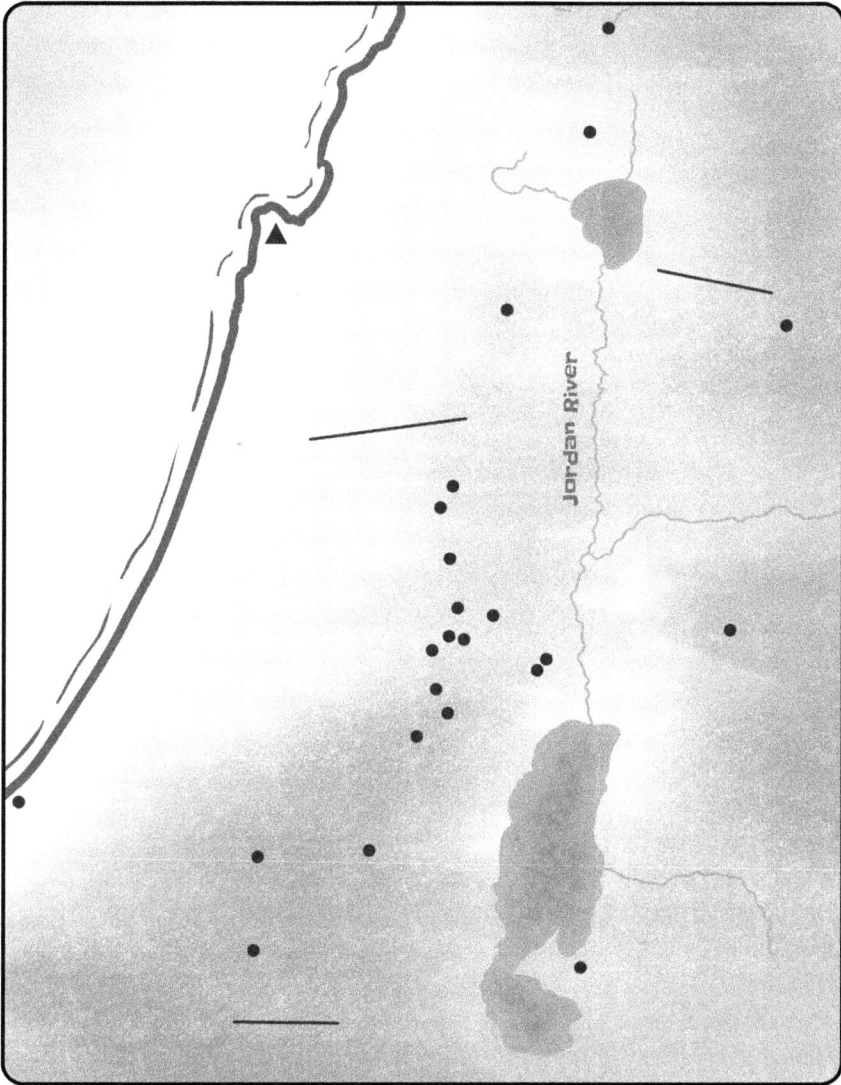

Jordan River

© Master the Bible Ministries

Answers in Appendix E Map 3

CHAPTER 29

Songs and Wisdom

Psalms and Proverbs

DIRECTIONS: Read the story to yourself. Or read it as a family with each person reading a different part aloud. When you come to a place name in **bold**, draw a musical instrument in that location on a map in Appendix E.

Worshiping God with Singing
Psalms 22, 23, 72, 148, 1 Chronicles 23, 25

KING DAVID: When I was a boy, I started worshiping God with music. My whole life I wrote songs to God. More than seventy of the songs I wrote are in the book of Psalms. That's almost half the book!

WORSHIP LEADER ASAPH: David chose my family—along with Heman's and Juduthan's families—to lead worship in the temple. We teach younger family members how to listen to God as they sing and play instruments.

WORSHIP LEADER HEMAN: Every day twelve singers and about 20 to 30 musicians serve in the temple in **Jerusalem**. Here is one of the praise songs we sing:

Prophetic Songs

New Testament writers saw the psalms as prophecies. Every song, especially the ones by or about the king, tell us about Jesus. Check out Psalm 22 (Jesus' death), Psalm 110 (Jesus as priest), Psalm 2 (Jesus as king), Psalm 45 (Jesus' marriage).

WORSHIP LEADER ASAPH: Praise the LORD! Praise him, all his angels! Praise him, sun and moon! Let them praise the name of the LORD because he made them. Praise him from the earth! Praise him, fire and snow! Praise him, all you sea creatures! Praise him, all you kings of the earth! His glory is over the heavens and the earth!

KING DAVID: Many of the songs I wrote were about difficult things I went through. I told God how bad I was feeling. Then I asked him to help me. Because I knew God would deliver me, I ended my songs by celebrating the great ending God was going to give me. Korah's descendants helped with the worship in the temple. Listen to them singing one of my songs:

KORAH'S DESCENDANTS: My God, my God, why have you left me all alone? I cry to you, but you don't answer me. Everyone who sees me makes fun of me. But I have trusted in you since I was born. My enemies laugh when I suffer. They're dividing up my clothes. They're rolling dice to see who takes them. LORD, don't stay far away! Hurry and help me! When someone who is suffering cries to God, God pays attention. The whole earth will remember and turn to the LORD. They will proclaim,"He has done it!"

KING SOLOMON: Some songs are about the king, like this one I wrote: "Give the king ability to judge fairly. May he defend the people who are taken advantage of. May righteousness and prosperity last forever in his kingdom. All the nations will be blessed through him."

WORSHIP LEADER HEMAN: Other songs give thanks to God or share wisdom about how to live well. Some songs just enjoy being with God. Here's a favorite:

KING DAVID: The LORD is my shepherd. I have everything I need. He gives me green pastures to lie down in. He leads me beside quiet waters. He gives my soul new strength. He guides me in the right path. Even though I walk through the darkest valley, I won't be afraid. You are with me. I know your goodness and love will be with me all my life. I'll live in your house forever.

Wisdom to Live Life Well

Proverbs 1-31

KING SOLOMON: I wrote a lot of proverbs or wise sayings. If you do what my proverbs advise, life will go better for you. You can find success, joy, and prosperity. Listen to some of the wise sayings mentioned most often.

PERSON 1: The kind of person you are will determine whether you are successful in life. God gives righteous people what they desire. But people who run after evil will die.

PERSON 2: Lazy people want a lot of things but never get them. But people who work hard have their desires fully satisfied.

PERSON 3: Your tongue has the power of life or death. Your words can heal like a life-giving tree. Or your words can break someone's spirit.

PERSON 1: People who spend too much time with wine have trouble and sorrow and pain they wouldn't otherwise have.

PERSON 2: Good friends make you a better person. They offer you help and advice. But don't become friends with angry or foolish people. They will bring their harm into your life.

PERSON 3: Don't trust in money. It can't save you when your soul is being judged. Use your money to be kind to the poor. Then you'll have a reward from God.

PERSON 1: Don't follow sexual temptation. It will lead to death.

PERSON 2: Keep following what your father taught you. Don't hate your mother when she is old. Your parents gave life to you. Honoring them will give you a long life.

PERSON 3: Don't do whatever seems best to you. Ask advice from others. Submit to discipline. Be willing to be corrected. Then you'll become a better person.

Wisdom

God set the natural world to work best when it follows the ways of heaven. So, when we're loving, generous, and respectful, things go better. Wisdom tells us what to do so we're following the best path in life.

KING SOLOMON: I hope you do more than read and memorize the wise sayings I wrote. I want you to become a wise person yourself. So in the first chapters of Proverbs, I tell you how I became a wise person. Then you can follow my path. You must begin by having respect for the LORD. Then—can you hear her? Wisdom is calling out in the streets:

WISDOM: I will tell you my thoughts! I will make you wise! I've built my house. I've prepared food and drink for you. Come inside and get to know me. Take my food and drink into your body. Then you will have my understanding inside you. It will make you wise and fill you with knowledge.

KING SOLOMON: I heard Wisdom calling. I developed a relationship with God's Wisdom. What made me wise wasn't studying. It wasn't thinking deeply about things. What gave me wisdom was my relationship with God. From our close relationship, God poured his understanding into my heart. Anyone can do the same thing! Anyone can become wise by growing close to God!

Review It!

Who wrote the most psalms? When did he start worshiping God?

Who did David put in charge of worship at the temple? How many singers and musicians served in the temple every day?

Who wrote a lot of Proverbs?

List three wise sayings from the book of Proverbs.

Remember It!

SONG: *Kings of Judah, Uzziah-Zedekiah*

Honors! Add What did the Kings Do? verses 7-8

Learn these timeline events.

33. Ahaz doesn't rely on God

34. God saves Jerusalem when Hezekiah prays

35. Manasseh acts wickedly then repents

36. Zephaniah, Habakkuk, and Jeremiah prophesy in Judah

Think About It!

Are all the Psalms praises to God? Name three other things Psalms can sing about.

What do you think the most important wisdom principle is? Why?

Many people can follow wisdom principles. But how do we become wise? What did Solomon do to become wise?

I am whole and complete in God.

Map It!

Dots show where cities are. Lines show where regions are. Label these places:

- Philistia
- Gath
- Ekron
- Ashdod
- Ashkelon
- Gaza

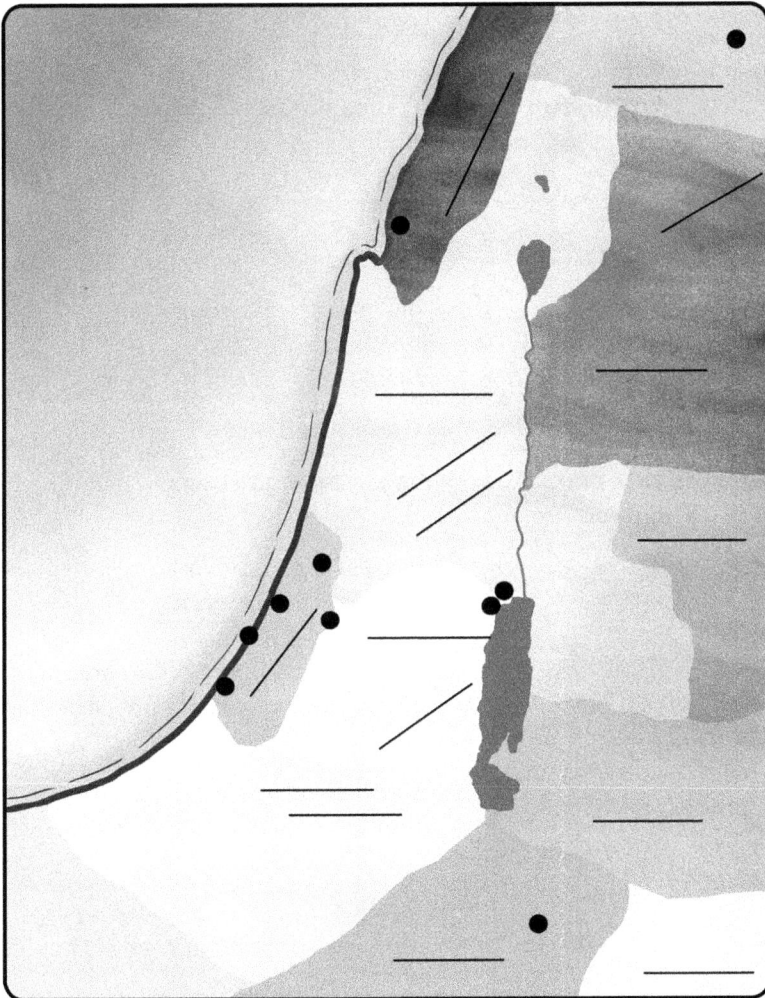

Answers in Appendix E Map 5

CHAPTER 30

More Wisdom Books

Song of Solomon, Ecclesiastes, Job

DIRECTIONS: Read the story to yourself. Or read it as a family with each person reading a different part aloud. When you come to a place name in **bold**, draw a heart in that location on a map in Appendix E.

God's Deep Love for Us
Song of Solomon 1-4

KING SOLOMON: I wrote an excellent love song! It talks about my marriage to my beautiful bride. But it also teaches us about how much God loves us.

BRIDE: I am dark and lovely. The king noticed me.

GROOM: You look beautiful with the jewelry I gave you. How truly lovely you are!

Love

God can't wait to spend time with you. He is delighted in you. You have stolen his heart. Being with God, loving him, is the most delightful thing. Nothing else compares to it.

BRIDE: He brought me to his hall for a banquet. He looked at me lovingly. Daughters of **Jerusalem**, don't stir up or awaken love until it's ready!

GROOM: My beautiful one, come away with me! Let me see your face. Let me hear your voice. Your voice is sweet. And your face is lovely.

CHORUS: See how glorious King Solomon looks on the day of his wedding—on the happiest day of his life!

BRIDE: My lover is mine and I am his. Until the dawn arrives and the shadows flee, we will be together.

GROOM: You have stolen my heart, my bride. You have stolen my heart by glancing at me. Your love is so delightful! It's much better than wine. Your perfume is better than any spice!

BRIDE: Hurry! Bring me into your bedroom chamber! Being with you is more delightful than anything else!

Wisdom and Suffering
Ecclesiastes 1-2, 8, 12; Job 1-42

Ecclesiastes

TEACHER: I'm David's son. I'm king in **Jerusalem**. I became much wiser than anyone else. So, I decided to take a careful look at everything to figure out what the meaning of life is.

PERSON 1: When you tried partying and doing whatever you wanted, what did you discover?

TEACHER: Partying is foolish. Doing whatever you want all the time doesn't bring anything good to your life. It's like chasing the wind—running after something you can't hold onto. Even if you caught it, it wouldn't give you anything at all.

PERSON 2: When you bought whatever you wanted, what did you find?

TEACHER: I bought myself whatever I wanted. I became very rich. In the end I realized none of that was worth anything.

PERSON 3: What should we do with our lives then?

TEACHER: Be happy and enjoy what God has given you. Enjoy all your work. These are gifts that God has given you.

PERSON 4: After you examined everything, what did you conclude? What is the best thing we can do?

Chasing the Wind

Have you ever tried to catch the wind? You can't hold onto it, can you? Even if you caught it, what would you be holding? Nothing! That's how Solomon felt about chasing after money and pleasure and success. They are easily gone. And even if we caught them, they would give us nothing. Only God gives meaning to life.

TEACHER: Respect God and keep his commandments. God will judge everything you do.

NARRATOR: Most people think the Teacher in Ecclesiastes is Solomon. They believe he used his great wisdom to think deeply about what gives life meaning. What did he conclude? The things most of us think will make us happy—money, stuff, getting whatever we want all the time—don't bring us satisfaction. Our souls were built to find their happiness in God. The closer we draw to God, the more satisfied we will be.

Job's Suffering

NARRATOR: Job was a righteous man. God blessed him so much that he had ten children and a lot of possessions. He was very wealthy. One day Satan told God:

SATAN: The only reason Job is serving you is because you have blessed him so much. Let me take away what he has. Let me make his life miserable. Then he will curse you.

GOD: All right. You can take away what he has. You can even make him sick. But you can't kill him.

NARRATOR: In a single day, Job lost all his children and property. Then painful boils appeared on Job's body. He was miserable day and night.

JOB: The LORD gives and the LORD takes away. Blessed be his name! Are we supposed to accept only what's good from God? Are we supposed to reject the bad things?

NARRATOR: Three of Job's closest friends heard about what had happened to him. Along with other friends, they came to comfort him. After spending seven days sitting with him, they started to speak. They had never seen a righteous person suffer so deeply. So, they assumed Job had done something to deserve the bad things.

FRIEND ELIPHAZ: Has an innocent person ever been punished? Tell God you're sorry for whatever you did. Then he will bless you again.

FRIEND ELIHU: Job, you say you haven't done anything wrong. But we know that God always warns us when we wander from him. If you didn't understand his first warnings, he would have given you another one. Surely he at least warned you in a dream.

NARRATOR: Job was so close to God that he could handle God taking everything from him. But when his friends blamed him for what had happened, Job reached his breaking point.

JOB: I am suffering innocently! Be kind to me. I know that after I die, I will see God with my own eyes. How I wish I could see him now! I wish I could present my case to him.

NARRATOR: Job was crying out for a kind of interaction with God he had never had before. He wanted to see God and speak with him. He wasn't satisfied with just offering him sacrifices and prayers from a distance. When we go through hard times, the purpose is often to grow in our desire for a deeper relationship with God—because our relationship with God is not enough to make us feel okay through the difficult time. God gave Job what he wanted. In a whirlwind, God called out to Job:

GOD: Where were you when I set the earth in place? Did you decide what the earth's measurements would be? Have you ever commanded the morning to come? Are the wild animals your servants?

JOB: How could I answer you? I know you can do anything. I had heard about you. But now my eyes have seen you. I repent—I change the way I think and act toward you.

GOD: I'm growing angry at your friends because they didn't speak what's right. Pray for them. Then I won't treat them as their foolishness deserves.

NARRATOR: After Job prayed for his friends, God restored to him twice as much as he had lost. He had double the riches. Ten more children were born to him. Job lived another 140 years—long enough to see his great-great grandchildren.

Why did God allow Satan to take everything away from Job? God didn't give Job a direct answer. But we can see how it changed his life. In the beginning of the story, Job thought he'd have to wait until he died to see God himself. Then the difficult things caused Job to desire more from God. He wanted to see and talk to God now. When God appeared to Job and talked with him, it changed how Job interacted with God.

No matter how close we are to God, we can be closer. God desires a deeper relationship with us. Sometimes God will allow us to go through difficult things so we can realize the limits of our relationship with him. He wants us to ask him for a deeper connection. Then God will bring us out of the hard times. God never intends for the difficult things to last forever. But he will use them to bring much good into our lives.

Review It!

What was Song of Solomon about?

Describe the Teacher in Ecclesiastes. Where did he live? What was he trying to do?

Why did Job's friends think he was suffering? Were they right?

What happened to Job in the beginning of the book? the middle? the end?

Remember It!

SONG: *Psalms*

Learn these timeline events.

37. Josiah's reforms
38. Daniel and Ezekiel are taken to Babylon
39. Judah falls to Babylon and is exiled

Think About It!

How does the Groom describe the Bride's face and voice in Song of Solomon? What does this description tell you about how God thinks of you?

What will make us satisfied in life according to Ecclesiastes? Why did he compare pleasure and riches and many other things to "chasing the wind"? What does this analogy show you?

Why did God allow Job to go through a difficult time? What was different in Job's life as a result of suffering?

I have captured God's heart.

Dots show where cities are. Lines show where regions are. Label these places:

- Moab
- Canaan

- Ammon
- Aram (Syria)

Answers in Appendix E Map 5

CHAPTER 31

Prophets to Israel

Amos, Hosea, Jonah, Obadiah, Joel

DIRECTIONS: Read the story to yourself. Or read it as a family with each person reading a different part aloud. When you come to a place name in **bold**, draw a bow and arrow in that location on a map in Appendix E.

Amos and Hosea Warn Israel

Amos

Amos 1-2, 4-5, 9

NARRATOR: Israel always had prophets. Since the very first king, prophets had an official position in the king's court. They were supposed to tell the king what God wanted them to do. In King Uzziah's time, some prophets started to write their prophecies in books that we still have today. Their messages weren't just for the people who first heard them. Their words also spoke to us. Amos and Hosea were among the first of these prophets.

AMOS: Trouble is coming for all the nations surrounding Israel—for **Syria**, **Philistia**, **Tyre**, **Edom**, **Ammon**, **Moab**, and **Judah**. They will be punished for the wicked things they have done to others. Trouble is also coming on Israel because they have mistreated the poor. They've worshiped idols.

ISRAELITE: Does God really want to punish us?

AMOS: God doesn't want to punish you. He wants you to return to him. God says, "I gave you no food to eat, but you didn't come back to me. I gave you no rain before harvest, but you didn't come back to me. I destroyed your crops with disease, but you didn't come back to me."

ISRAELITE: When our ancestors faced those things, they prayed to God to help them. But we have asked idols to rescue us. We haven't cared about God.

AMOS: If you don't come back to God, he will destroy the nation. You will be forced to leave the land.

NARRATOR: The priest at Bethel, the place where Israel worshiped a golden calf, didn't like what Amos had to say. He tried to make the king angry with Amos and he said:

PRIEST AMAZIAH: Go away, Amos! Run back to Judah! Don't prophesy at Bethel anymore!

AMOS: The disasters I've talked about will happen to your family, Amaziah. They will happen in your own lifetime.

NARRATOR: People didn't listen to Amos. They didn't come back to God. God would discipline them. But after the discipline, there was good news.

AMOS: God says, "In the future, I'll bring my people back to Israel. They will rebuild the cities. I'll plant them in the land, and they'll never be uprooted again."

Prophets

God gave Israel prophets so everyone—from the king to regular people—could know what God had to say. When we wonder what God's opinion is, just ask him. "God, what do you want me to know today?" is a great question.

Hosea

Hosea 1-3

NARRATOR: About a decade after Amos, Hosea began prophesying in **Israel**. As a prophet, Hosea's life was a living picture of God's relationship with Israel. So, God told him:

GOD: Marry a woman who will be unfaithful to you. I am married to Israel spiritually, and they are unfaithful to me.

NARRATOR: Hosea married Gomer. She was unfaithful to Hosea and eventually left him. Now the nation could see how it broke God's heart when they prayed to idols rather than to him. After some time passed, God told Hosea:

GOD: Show love to your wife again. She loves another man and continually is unfaithful to you. But I love Israel even though they turn to other gods.

HOSEA: Gomer, I paid a lot of money to buy you back. You must live with me and be faithful to me. And I will wait for you.

NARRATOR: God was giving a living picture of what he would do. Jesus would pay a huge price so we could live with God again.

Prophets Jonah, Obadiah, & Joel Speak Amazing Messages

Jonah

Jonah 1-4

NARRATOR: Jonah prophesied in the reign of Jeroboam II of Israel. He had an adventure delivering a message to **Nineveh**, the capital of **Assyria**.

GOD told Jonah:

GOD: Go to Nineveh. Tell them my judgment is coming because they've been wicked.

JONAH: What if I tell them God's message? They may change! Because God is full of mercy, he won't punish them if they stop doing wicked things. So, I won't preach to them. I'll run in the opposite direction!

NARRATOR: Jonah boarded a ship to sail far away from Ninevah. Once the boat was at sea, God sent a huge storm. The sailors were sure they'd die. Jonah told them:

JONAH: I'm running away from God. That's why he sent this storm. Throw me into the sea, and it will be calm.

NARRATOR: Although the sailors didn't want to, they threw Jonah overboard. He almost drowned. Then God sent a huge fish to swallow him. Inside the fish, Jonah prayed:

JONAH: I thank you, God, for rescuing me. Anyone can receive your mercy.

NARRATOR: God commanded the fish to spit Jonah onto dry land. Again, God told Jonah:

GOD: Go to Nineveh, and announce my message.

JONAH: Listen, Nineveh! In 40 days, you will be destroyed!

KING OF NINEVEH: Don't eat or drink anything—not even your farm animals should eat or drink! Stop doing wicked things! Maybe God will be kind to us.

NARRATOR: When God saw that they had changed, he had pity on them. He didn't destroy them.

JONAH: Isn't this exactly what I thought you would do, God? I'm so angry that you were kind to Nineveh.

GOD: Do you have a right to be angry? Nineveh is a large city with a lot of people. They can't tell right from wrong. Shouldn't I be concerned for them—and for all the animals, too?

Father

Jonah ran away from God. He had immature attitudes. But God never said he was angry with Jonah. Like a Father training a child, God was trying to show Jonah the "adult" perspective. God isn't upset with us for being immature. He cherishes us at every spiritual age—just like a true dad.

Obadiah's Message about Edom

Obadiah

NARRATOR: This short prophesy isn't dated. Obadiah spoke to **Edom**, telling them that they would regret being mean to **Jerusalem** when it lost a battle.

OBADIAH: Edom, you shouldn't have laughed at Jerusalem when it was destroyed. You shouldn't have marched through the gates and stolen its wealth. You shouldn't have captured people fleeing the city and turned them over to their enemies.

EDOM: No one can bring me down!

OBADIAH: People will do to you what you have done to them. You'll be paid back for what you've done. I'll save some of my people and they will return to the land. Israelites from the **Negev** will take over Edom's mountains. Israelites will possess **Philistia**, **Ephraim**, **Samaria**, and **Gilead**. Jerusalem will rule over Edom. The kingdom will belong to God.

Joel Tells what the Locust Invasion Meant

NARRATOR: Joel's book is undated. It talks about a locust invasion that destroyed the crops. Joel wanted to know what the locust invasion meant spiritually. God gave him this message:

JOEL: Has anything like this ever happened? Four types of locust ate everything in the land! Like an army, they invaded us. They show us what the day of the LORD will be like. It will be a day of darkness. A huge and powerful army will invade like fire! Who can survive it?

PERSON 1: What should we do?

JOEL: "Return to me with all your heart," God says. Don't eat anything. Call everyone together to pray. God is full of love and slow to anger. Perhaps he will be kind to us. Maybe he'll leave a blessing behind.

PERSON 2: Have pity on us, Lord!

JOEL: God says, "I will give back to you what the locusts ate. You will have plenty of food. Don't be afraid! Rejoice and be glad! I will pour out my Spirit on everyone. Your sons and daughters will prophesy. Your old men will have dreams from God. The sun will turn dark, and the moon will be blood red. On that day, everyone who calls on the name of the LORD will be saved!"

Review It!

What was the main message of Amos?

What did Hosea's marriage tell people about God?

How did Jonah act immaturely—more like a baby than an adult?

What animal invaded the land in Joel's time? What did Joel compare them to?

Remember It!

SONG: *Wisdom Books*

Learn these timeline events.

40. Temple is destroyed
41. Remnant returns and rebuilds the Temple
42. Haggai and Zechariah prophesy

Think About It!

Why do you think God punished Israel? What did God want them to gain from the discipline?

Thinking about how Hosea bought Gomer back, how much does God love you—even if you've done bad things?

What did Edom do wrong? What does Obadiah's prophecy tell us about how we should treat people who are our enemies?

God loves me so much he would pay any price for me.

Map It!

Label these places on the map in the next chapter.

- Edom
- Bozrah
- Jebusites
- Hivites

CHAPTER 32

Prophets to Judah

Isaiah and Micah

DIRECTIONS: Read the story to yourself. Or read it as a family with each person reading a different part aloud. When you come to a place name in **bold**, draw a shield in that location on a map in Appendix E.

Isaiah Prophecies to Kings Ahaz and Hezekiah
Isaiah 1, 6-7, 36-39, 58, 65-66

NARRATOR: Isaiah prophesied in **Judah** during the reigns of Uzziah, Jotham, Ahaz, and Hezekiah. His book is divided into two main parts. The first half of the book centers around two times Judah faced an invasion—one when Ahaz was king and one when Hezekiah was king. The second half of the book promises that God will give back to his people every good thing that they lost.

ISAIAH: I also warned people that they should make God their first priority. People think that if they go to a religious service or give money to God, then he is satisfied. But what matters to God is people's hearts. He's not impressed if people go to the temple, but then treat other people badly.

In the year Uzziah died, I saw God seated on a throne high up. Seraphs—winged creatures—hovered above him, shouting:

SERAPHS: Holy, holy, holy is the Lord who commands armies! The whole earth is full of his glory!

NARRATOR: The sound of their voices shook the door frames, and the temple was filled with smoke. Then God said:

GOD: Who will go work for me? Whom should I send?

ISAIAH: Here I am! Send me!

GOD: Go tell these people, "Listen, but don't understand." Make their eyes blind and their hearts hard. Otherwise, they may change and be healed.

NARRATOR: Isaiah's first job was to release a spirit of blindness on God's people. The blindness prevented them from understanding what was going on in the spiritual world. This spirit of blindness was still on God's people when Jesus came 700 years later. It caused people to not recognize who Jesus was (Matthew 13:13-16). God wanted Jesus to be rejected and killed—and rise from death. Although spiritual blindness seems bad, it was important for God's plan to redeem his people.

ISAIAH: When Ahaz was king, **Syria** and **Israel** planned to invade Judah and end David's dynasty. God told me, 'Tell Ahaz this plan won't happen." Then God told Ahaz to ask him for a sign. God wanted him to be certain that David's dynasty would rule from **Jerusalem**. But Ahaz was afraid. He said:

KING AHAZ: I won't test God by asking him for a sign.

ISAIAH: God himself will give you a sign. The virgin will give birth to a son. You'll call his name Immanuel. (That means "God is with us.")

NARRATOR: God quoted this prophecy to Mary, Jesus' mother, when God told her she would give birth to Jesus.

Blindness

When people don't understand your faith, it's okay. They're probably suffering from spiritual blindness—not being able to see what God is doing. That just makes your faith more special. It's something that only a few people can see and understand.

ISAIAH: Even though Ahaz didn't trust God, Judah was saved. During Hezekiah's rule, Jerusalem faced another danger. The king of **Assyria** threatened to defeat Jerusalem. He claimed to be more powerful than Judah's God.

KING HEZEKIAH: I've asked Isaiah to pray for us. I know our God is the only true God. I know he can save us.

ISAIAH: Here's what God says, "Because you obeyed God and trusted in him, God will save you from Assyria. Don't worry about them. They won't even shoot an arrow at the city."

NARRATOR: In the middle of the night, an angel of God struck down 185,000 soldiers in the Assyrian camp. The next morning the rest of the army packed up and left.

ISAIAH: God saved Jerusalem. He also saved Hezekiah's life. At that time, Hezekiah was very sick. When he cried to God to heal him, God told me that he would live.

NARRATOR: Isaiah wrote many prophecies about God's Savior. He was also the first prophet to talk about the new heaven and new earth. He explained that God would restore everything that humanity had lost by turning away from God. We would live in a perfect place with God again!

Micah

Micah 1-7, Jeremiah 26:18-19

NARRATOR: Micah prophesied at the same time as Isaiah.

MICAH: God is coming out of his palace! The mountains will melt before him! He's coming because of **Judah**'s rebellion! The nation has set up idols in Jerusalem. I will weep. I will howl like a wild dog. **Jerusalem** will be a pile of ruins. The temple will be a hill filled with weeds.

RICH PERSON: I dream about how I will take advantage of the poor.

MICAH: You take widows' houses away from them. You cheat people out of their property. So, a disaster will come on this nation. Your houses and fields will be given to the nation who conquers you. You won't have land in God's community.

CHILD: When I go to the market, I can't buy enough food for my family to eat.

MICAH: God says, "I won't overlook the unfair scales in the market. Traders use them to sell people less food than they paid you for. Because they cheated others out of their food, the sellers won't have enough to eat!"

NARRATOR: Why would God let the nation be conquered? He wanted to correct the wrong things people were doing to the poor. By judging the sins of the nation, God would show mercy to the poor. But God didn't want to destroy Judah. He wanted them to listen to Micah—and change.

KING HEZEKIAH: I've heard what Micah has been preaching. LORD, please don't destroy us. I will remove the idols in Jerusalem. I will turn the nation back to you.

NARRATOR: God listened to Hezekiah's prayer. He saw the reforms Hezekiah did. Because of Hezekiah's obedience, God supernaturally rescued the nation from **Assyria**. Micah's prophecies helped save the

nation! They alerted the king to how serious the situation was. They showed Hezekiah what he needed to do to avoid God's punishment. Micah's book is also full of hope.

MICAH: In the future, people from many nations will stream to the temple. It will be more important than any other government on earth. God will instruct people from **Zion** (that's Jerusalem). There will be peace on earth. People will turn their swords into plows to use for farming. Nations won't train for war anymore. God will throw people's sins into the deepest part of the sea.

Hope

Hope is being excited about what God has promised—even when it hasn't happened yet. Micah told people about the good ending God had planned. He saw that ending. He wanted people to hope even when everything around them was discouraging.

Review It!

What was the first message God told Isaiah to preach?

What was one prophecy Isaiah gave about Jesus?

What things were people doing to the poor that Micah preached against?

What bad thing did Micah say would happen to the temple? What good thing did he say would happen to it?

SONG: *Major Prophets*

Learn these timeline events.

43. Esther saves Jews in Persia

44. Ezra and Nehemiah return to Judah

45. Malachi prophesies

Think About It!

In Micah's prophecies, how would God's judgment of the nation impact the rich and poor differently? Who would be better off? Who would be worse off?

What was similar in the stories about Ahaz and Hezekiah facing an invasion? What was different about them?

When is spiritual blindness bad? When is it good?

God has an amazing plan for my life.

Map It!

Dots show where cities are. Lines show where regions are. Label these places and people groups:

- Perrizites
- Hittites
- Bashan

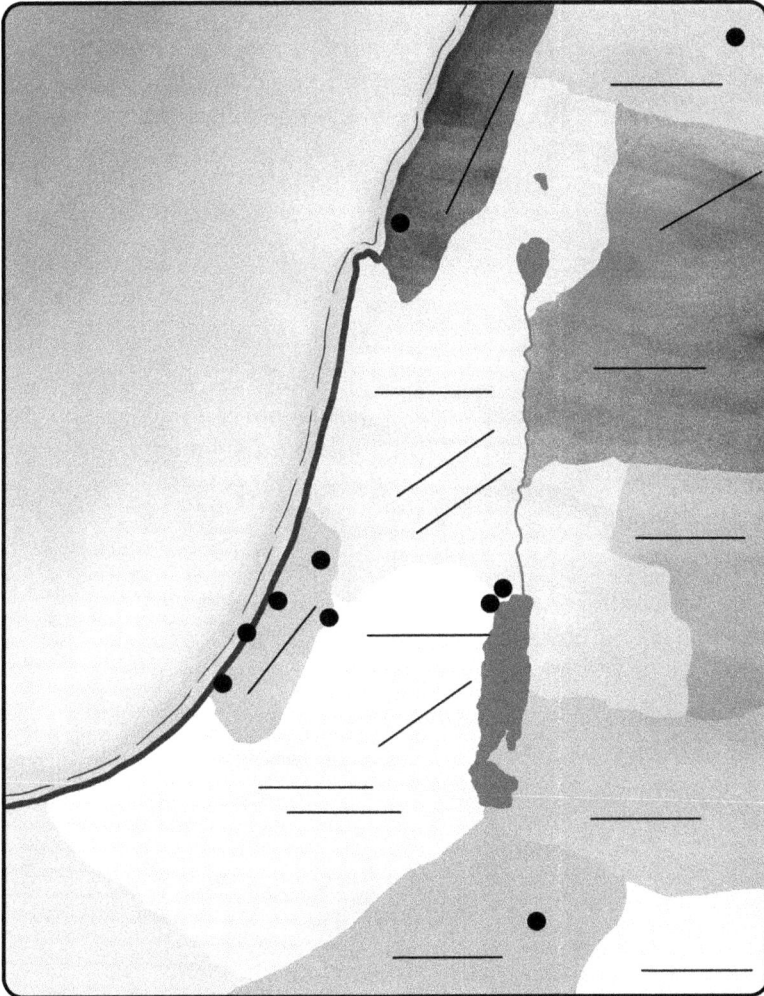

Answers in Appendix E Map 5

CHAPTER 33

Prophets to the Last Kings

Zephaniah, Nahum, Habakkuk, Jeremiah

DIRECTIONS: Read the story to yourself. Or read it as a family with each person reading a different part aloud. When you come to a place name in **bold**, draw a hammer in that location on a map in Appendix E.

Zephaniah, Nahum, Habakkuk Try to Save the Kingdom

Zephaniah

Zephaniah 1, 3; 2 Kings 23

NARRATOR: Zephaniah prophesied in **Jerusalem** during Josiah's reign. Many people think he motivated King Josiah to turn the nation back to God. His prophecies helped to save **Judah**!

ZEPHANIAH: The LORD says, "I will destroy everything from the face of the earth! I will attack Judah and Jerusalem! I will remove from this place every trace of idol worship! I will punish the princes. They are as fierce as lions."

KING JOSIAH: Remove all the idols from Jerusalem! Smash them up! I will turn the nation back to the LORD!

ZEPHANIAH: Shout for joy, Jerusalem! The LORD has removed the judgment against you! The LORD is with you! He is so mighty he can save you. He will delight in you. He will be with you quietly in his love. He will sing for joy because of you.

Nahum's Message about Nineveh

Nahum 1, 3

NARRATOR: Nahum's book is undated, but many people think he prophesied around the same time as Zephaniah. He had a message for **Nineveh**, the capital of **Assyria**, about 150 years after Jonah preached there. This time, destruction of Nineveh seemed unavoidable.

NAHUM: It takes a long time for the LORD to get angry. But he will certainly punish wicked people. The LORD is good. He protects everyone who runs to him for help. But with a powerful flood he will destroy Nineveh. He will chase his enemies into darkness.

KING OF ASSYRIA: We are powerful! We have many soldiers!

Did God change his mind?

God saved Nineveh when Jonah preached. Why did Nahum prophesy the city's destruction? A long time had passed. The king of Assyria didn't humble himself. He had been cruel to many nations. Now it was time for him to be treated like he had treated others.

NAHUM: The LORD has decided, "Your dynasty will end. I will destroy all your idols and their temples." Everyone who hears about your destruction will clap their hands for joy. They'll be glad because you were always cruel to other nations.

Habakkuk Listens to God

Habakkuk 1-3

NARRATOR: Habakkuk's book isn't dated. Many people think he prophesied not long after Nahum, about the same time as Jeremiah. He saw how sinful the people of Judah were acting and wondered if God was going to fix the problem.

HABAKKUK: How long am I going to have to tell you, God, about the wicked things people around me are doing? How long will it take you to do something about it?

GOD: You'll be shocked at what I'm about to do. I'm going to empower the Babylonians, that mean and greedy nation. They're going to sweep across the earth, capturing nations. They'll punish Jerusalem.

HABAKKUK: Why will you use a nation even more wicked than Judah to correct Judah's problems? That would make things much worse than what we're suffering now. I'm going to keep watching until I hear your answer.

GOD: I will use **Babylon** to correct Judah. Then Babylon will have to pay for the wrong they do. Because they destroyed many nations, they will also be destroyed.

NARRATOR: At first Habakkuk didn't understand God's solution to this problem. He thought the cure was worse than what he was suffering. Then he realized God's way would solve the root of the problem. He learned to thank God for hard times and easy times. God used both to bring us into the best for our lives.

HABAKKUK: I am awed by you, LORD! You are so powerful. You stomp on the nations. I will praise you when you protect us. And I will praise you in difficult times. I will be happy because of the God who saves me! You are my strength!

Jeremiah Predicts Judah's Fall   Jeremiah 1, 9, 13, 25, 29, 37, 52

NARRATOR: The LORD spoke to Jeremiah from Josiah's reign until after **Jerusalem** fell to the **Babylonians**.

GOD: Before you were born, I set you apart to be a prophet.

JEREMIAH: Oh, Lord, I am too young to know how to speak well.

GOD: Don't say, "I'm too young." I will give you the words to say. Don't be afraid because I will protect you.

NARRATOR: In Josiah's reign, the king listened to Jeremiah. But every king after Josiah didn't pay attention to what Jeremiah was preaching.

JEREMIAH: The LORD says, "I will send a nation **Judah**! Unless you repent, Jerusalem will be destroyed!"

NARRATOR: People didn't change what they were doing. When the Babylonians came to attack Judah, Jeremiah told people to surrender to them. Many leaders thought Jeremiah was a traitor. They tried to kill him. They put him in prison several times.

JEREMIAH: All I ever experience is trouble and sadness! I could cry all day long!

NARRATOR: Following God's path was difficult for Jeremiah. People didn't like his prophecies. They treated him meanly. But in the end, it was the best path for him. The people in Jerusalem who didn't listen to Jeremiah suffered from famine and war. But God saved Jeremiah. When Jerusalem fell to the Babylonians, something amazing happened for him.

BABYLONIAN CAPTAIN: The LORD your God brought disaster against Jerusalem because your people sinned. Jeremiah, today I will set you free from prison. If you want to come to Babylon with me, I will take care of you. If you'd rather stay here, you may. You can go anywhere in the land you want to go.

JEREMIAH: I'll stay in Judah. I'll help the person the king of Babylon left in charge of the land.

Destiny

God's plan for our lives isn't our idea. It's something God placed inside us before we were born. We find our destiny by talking to God about who he made us—the talents and personality he gave us.

NARRATOR: Jeremiah was very sad that Jerusalem was destroyed. Most people think he wrote the book Lamentations—a sad song about the defeat. Because Jeremiah obeyed God, he was saved from the disaster. God told Jeremiah that Jerusalem wouldn't remain defeated forever.

JEREMIAH: The nation will go into exile in Babylon. After 70 years, God will bring you back!

Review It!

Which king did Zephaniah prophecy to? Did that king listen?

What nation did Nahum prophecy about? Did he share good or bad news?

What nation did God tell Habakkuk was going to punish Judah? Why did that news surprise Habakkuk?

What are some bad things that happened to Jeremiah? How did God save him in the end?

Remember It!

SONG: *Minor Prophets 12* (part 1) and *Patriarchs and Matriarchs*

Bonus! Minor Prophets Message verse 1

Learn these patriarchs and matriarchs of Israel.

- Abraham and Sarah
- Isaac and Rebecca
- Jacob, Leah, and Rachel

Think About It!

Why did God save Nineveh when Jonah preached, and then destroy Nineveh after Nahum prophesied?

When did God set his plans for Jeremiah's life? If God made his plans for us before we were born, are God's plans based on whether we're a good person or are they based on who he made us?
Will God's plans for us change if we make a mistake?

Why was God's plan for Jeremiah's life the best—even though it included difficult things?

God's plan for my life is unchangeable
I cannot lose it even if I make a mistake.

Map It!

Dots show where cities are. Lines show where regions are. Label these places:

- Babylonia/Chaldea
- Ur
- Babylon
- Euphrates River (Great River)
- Tigris River

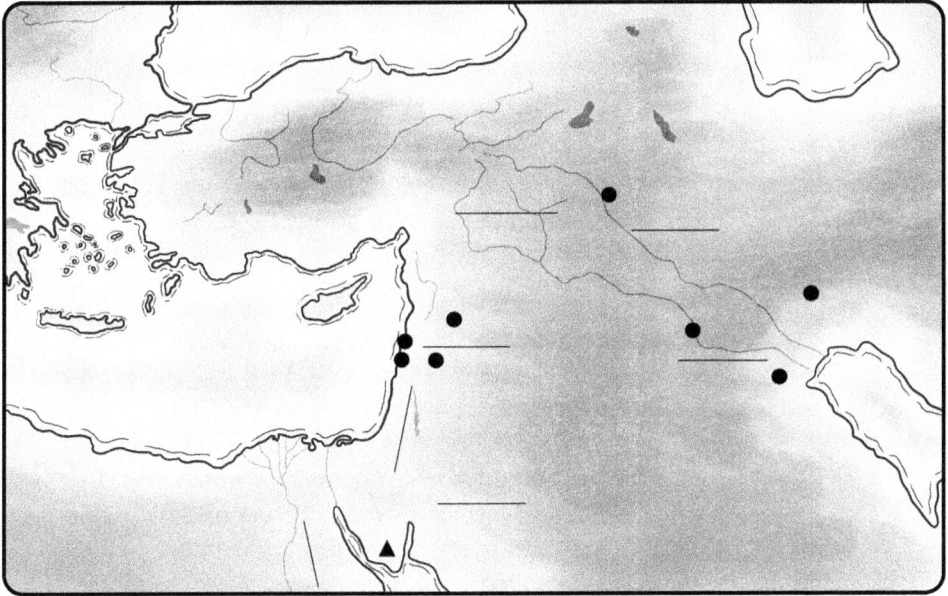

Answers in Appendix E Map 6

CHAPTER 34

Exile Prophets

Ezekiel, Daniel

DIRECTIONS: Read the story to yourself. Or read it as a family with each person reading a different part aloud. When you come to a place name in **bold**, draw a fire in that location on a map in Appendix E.

Ezekiel Encounters God

Ezekiel 1-4, 8-12, 20, 40-48

NARRATOR: Ezekiel was taken captive with King Jehoiachin (and Daniel) about twelve years before **Jerusalem** fell to the Babylonians. God called him to be a prophet to the exiles in **Babylon**. His book centers around three amazing encounters he had with God and the cherubim—special angels who stand near God's throne.

EZEKIEL: I noticed a storm coming with fire and lightning flashes. As it drew nearer, I saw four living beings. They sort of looked like humans. But they had four faces and four wings. Each had the face of a person, a lion, an ox, and an eagle. Each had two wings spread out above, touching each other. Above their wings was a crystal platform. On that platform was a throne and someone sitting on the throne. He looked like fire with bright light shining out like a rainbow around him. When I saw him, I fell face down.

GOD: Son of man, I am sending you to speak my words to your own people. They will not listen to you. Don't worry about how they respond. Your job is just to speak my words.

EZEKIEL: For about seven years God told me to act out what he planned to do to Jerusalem. I wrote "Jerusalem" on a brick. Then I built siege ramps against it. I posted soldiers around it. I ate a limited diet for over a year as I lay on my side acting out the punishment on Israel and Judah. Another time, I dug a hole in the wall and crawled through it.

I was showing people how the king planned to escape the siege—but how he'd be captured.

NARRATOR: Ezekiel had another encounter with God and the cherubim.

EZEKIEL: God's Spirit took me in a vision to Jerusalem. He showed me how people were worshiping idols right in the LORD's temple. They thought God couldn't see what they were doing. They thought God would never punish them. But God showed me how he planned to destroy the city because of the evil things people were doing. God also showed me how he would protect all the people who didn't worship idols. I saw the glory of the LORD and the same living beings I saw when I first met God.

Ezekiel's Living Example

Ezekiel lay on his side tied up with ropes for over a year to show people how God would punish Israel. He did other difficult things for God. Why? Interacting with God changed him. Although he suffered, he gained something greater. Giving up comfortable things for God drew him closer to God in a way that lasted into eternity.

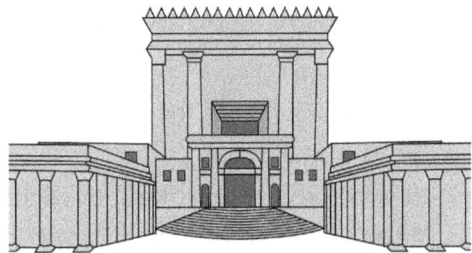

NARRATOR: The living beings, also called cherubim, lifted up their wings and moved toward the east gate of the temple with God's glory above them. God was leaving his temple. Without God's presence in the temple, it could be destroyed. God explained to Ezekiel why he was going to send people away from Jerusalem. The Israelites had a plan:

ISRAELITE: We will be like other nations. We'll worship idols made of wood and stone.

GOD: I will use my powerful hand to stop your plan. I will bring you out of Jerusalem and change you. Later I will bring you back, and you will serve me.

EZEKIEL: The Babylonians did set siege to Jerusalem, just like I acted out. They did capture the king and destroy the temple. They brought the survivors to Babylon. Then God gave me encouraging messages.

GOD: Even though the nation is like dry bones, I will make them live again.

EZEKIEL: Twenty years after I first saw God and the cherubim, I had a final encounter with God. In a vision God brought me to Israel and showed me in detail a new city and new temple. I saw the glory of the LORD coming into the temple by the east gate. His glory looked like how I had seen it in my first vision. The name of the city will be "The LORD is There."

Daniel Hears God
Daniel 1, 3, 7-12

NARRATOR: Daniel was the son of nobility in **Judah**. When he was very young, he was taken captive to **Babylon**. Trained to be a royal advisor, Daniel served several kings—from Nebuchadnezzar all the way to Cyrus, the Persian king who defeated Babylon.

DANIEL: I held important positions in the government. With God's help, I could interpret dreams, too. When I was older, I began having my own dreams from God. God showed me how the governments of this world would one day be given to God's people. They would rule the earth.

NARRATOR: The first part of Daniel's book shares adventures that he or his friends had as advisors to the king—like the time Daniel's friends Hananiah, Mishael, and Azariah were thrown into a fire by King Nebuchadnezzar. (Their Babylonian names were Shadrach, Meshach, and Abednego.)

KING NEBUCHADNEZZAR: Everyone must bow down to the huge statue I built. Whoever does not bow down will be thrown into a fire!

BABYLONIAN PERSON: O king, these three Jewish men who help Daniel govern Babylon won't bow down to your statue.

KING NEBUCHADNEZZAR: Is it true you won't bow down?

SHADRACH (ALSO CALLED HANANIAH): Our God is able to rescue us from your fire. But if not, then we want you to know that we won't serve your gods.

NARRATOR: Enraged, Nebuchadnezzar ordered the furnace turned up seven times hotter. Then he ordered Daniel's three friends to be thrown into it. Before long, the king couldn't believe what he saw.

KING NEBUCHADNEZZAR: Didn't we throw three men into the fire? I see four men walking around, unharmed! The fourth one looks like a god! Come out! Come here!

NARRATOR: Daniel's friends walked out of the fire. Their hair wasn't burned. Their clothes weren't damaged. They didn't even smell like smoke.

KING NEBUCHADNEZZAR: Praise be to your God! Only he can save!

NARRATOR: Rescuing Daniel's friends from the fire was just one miraculous thing Daniel wrote about in the first part of his book. In the second half, Daniel told about the dreams and visions God gave him.

DANIEL: God gave me several dreams and visions where I saw the kingdoms that would rule over the beautiful land. (That's what God called Israel in my visions.) First, Babylon would have control. Then Persia would defeat Babylon. Then the Persians would fall to **Greece**. Finally, a fourth kingdom would arise. The name of the fourth kingdom was never mentioned to me. At the end of the fourth kingdom, God would open a court session. He would sit as Judge. Here is what the court will decide:

ONE STANDING NEAR GOD: God will rule in favor of his holy ones. The authority and greatness of all the kingdoms under heaven will be given to God's people. God's kingdom is eternal.

Fifth Kingdom

What is the most important part of a story? The ending. It doesn't matter if it's difficult in the middle. How it ends is what counts. Earth's history finishes with God's holy ones ruling. Everything that ever happens on earth ends with God winning and his people ruling. Their last, fifth kingdom is the most important part of the visions Daniel saw.

DANIEL: I didn't always understand what God showed me. So, I would ask someone in the vision to explain it to me. Sometimes they told me the meaning. Sometimes they said I didn't need to understand. The visions were for a future time.

MAN IN LINEN CLOTHES: Seal the book, Daniel, until the time of the end. You will rest. Then at the end of days you will rise up. You'll receive what God has set aside for you.

Review It!

Who and what did Ezekiel see in his visions? Draw a picture of the living beings using Ezekiel's description.

What did Ezekiel do to act out his prophecies? What did those actions mean?

Who did Nebuchadnezzar throw in the fire and why?

What were the five kingdoms that would rule over Israel in Daniel's visions?

Remember It!

SONG: *Minor Prophets 12* (part 2) and *12 Tribes* (part 1)

Bonus! Minor Prophets Message verse 2

Learn six of the 12 tribes.

- Reuben
- Simeon
- Levi

- Judah
- Dan
- Naphtali

Think About It!

How were Ezekiel and Daniel similar? How were they different?

Ezekiel saw two visions of the temple. Where did he see God exiting the temple? Where did he see God returning to the temple? Was else was similar about the visions?

Which of the kingdoms Daniel saw was given an eternal kingdom? Which kingdom was most important? Why?

God loves me so much he plans to make me a ruler over the earth.

Map It!

Dots show where cities are. Lines show where regions are. Label these places:

- Susa
- Egypt
- Nile River
- Red Sea
- Mount Sinai

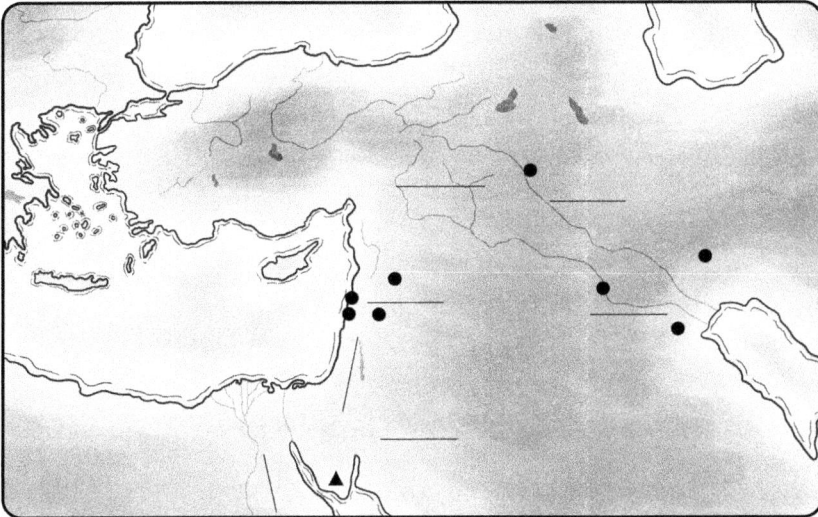

© Master the Bible Ministries

Answers in Appendix E Map 6

CHAPTER 35

After the Exile

Ezra, Haggai, Zechariah, Esther

DIRECTIONS: Read the story to yourself. Or read it as a family with each person reading a different part aloud. When you come to a place name in **bold**, draw a temple or house in that location on a map in Appendix E.

Jews Return and Rebuild the Temple

Ezra 1-6, Haggai 1-2, Zechariah 1-6, 8, 14

NARRATOR: Just as Jeremiah prophesied, the exile to **Babylon** lasted 70 years. When Persia defeated Babylon, Persian King Cyrus issued a decree:

KING CYRUS: The LORD God has given me all the kingdoms on earth. He told me to build a temple for him in **Jerusalem**. Any of God's people may return to **Judah** and rebuild the temple. I'll give you all the gold and silver articles King Nebuchadnezzar took from the temple.

NARRATOR: Almost 50,000 people returned to Judah. Zerubbabel, one of David's descendants, lead the group along with the priest Joshua. When the workers finished the foundation of the temple, everyone had a huge celebration. Then the local people began to oppose the rebuilding of the temple. They wrote a letter to the new Persian King Artaxerxes:

LOCAL PERSON: King, the Jews are rebuilding Jerusalem. If they finish, they will stop paying taxes to you. That city has rebelled many times in the past. You will lose control of this part of your country if they finish rebuilding.

KING: I've read your letter. I looked into the matter and discovered that Jerusalem has been ruled by powerful kings. They must stop their work. No one is permitted to rebuild until I say so.

NARRATOR: So, the work on the temple stopped for many years. When a new king came to power, prophets Haggai and Zechariah encouraged people to finish rebuilding the temple.

PROPHET HAGGAI: God says, "You work hard, but you don't have enough to eat. You put on clothes, but you aren't warm. You earn money, but there are holes in your money bag. Why? Because my temple remains in ruins. Rebuild my temple, and I will bless you! I am with you!"

PROPHET ZECHARIAH: God gave me eight visions in one night. God showed me that he will rebuild the temple and Jerusalem. His Spirit will empower Zerubbabel. God will crown the priest Joshua. His future plans for us are amazing! He will take away our sin in one day! He will give us the right to walk in heaven with him!

NARRATOR: With the prophets' encouragement, the people began rebuilding the temple. Before long, the local governor sent a letter to King Darius, the new Persian king. The governor wanted the king to stop the Jews.

GOVERNOR: King, the temple is being rebuilt in Jerusalem. The Jews claim King Cyrus gave them permission. Check in the royal record and let us know if that is true.

KING DARIUS: I found a scroll that says King Cyrus did order the temple in Jerusalem to be rebuilt. So now take the taxes that you collect and give them to the people rebuilding the temple. Give them everything they need. I want them to pray for me from their temple.

Worthy

Why was it important to rebuild the temple? Why couldn't people just worship God privately? God is worthy. He is worthy of public, crowded, joyful worship. He is worthy of daily, national, official worship. He is worthy of a gathering place so beautiful we could stare at it all day. He is worthy of a temple!

NARRATOR: The people were so excited God had changed the king's opinion. They worked hard to finish the temple. Finally, they were done! About twenty years had passed since they had started the work, but the temple was ready for worship!

ISRAELITE MAN: When we dedicated the temple, we offered hundreds of sacrifices. Then we celebrated Passover and Unleavened Bread together for one week. We were so happy!

ISRAELITE WOMAN: Some of us remembered the temple King Nebuchadnezzar destroyed. This temple didn't look as beautiful. But God had given us joy. It was wonderful to worship him in his temple again. He is worthy!

PROPHET HAGGAI: In the future, this temple will be more glorious than the old temple.

PROPHET ZECHARIAH: Riches from many nations will flow to the temple. In the future, many nations will come to worship the LORD, the King, at his temple. They will come to Jerusalem to celebrate the Feast of Tents. Many people and powerful nations will come to ask God's favor here.

Esther saves her People
Esther 1-9

NARRATOR: When Daniel and Ezekiel were taken captive to **Babylon**, so were the ancestors of Hadassah (that is Esther). They stayed in Babylon a long time. When King Cyrus permitted the Jews to return to **Judah**, Hadassah's family decided not to go with them. Perhaps twenty years or so after the temple was rebuilt in **Jerusalem**, Hadassah was born. After her parents died, her cousin Mordecai raised her. Then King Ahasuerus (or Xerxes) of Persia was looking for a new queen. He gathered all the beautiful young women to his palace. He would pick one to be queen.

MORDECAI: Hadassah, the king's men have come to take you to the palace. Go with them. Don't tell them you're a Jew. Use your Persian name, Esther.

NARRATOR: Obediently, Esther did everything that Mordecai and the king's men advised her to do. When it was time to be presented to the king, he loved Esther more than all the other women. With great joy, he chose her to be his queen. Meanwhile, the king promoted a rich man named Haman to a high position. When Haman saw that Mordecai wasn't bowing down to him, he grew very angry.

HAMAN: Mordecai isn't bowing to me! It is too small a thing to kill only Mordecai. I will kill all the Jews! I will cast a pur—a lot, sort of like dice—to decide which day and month we will kill them!

NARRATOR: The lot chose a date eleven months away. The king gave Haman permission to make a law that anywhere in his kingdom—from India to Ethiopia—people could kill the Jews and take their property on that day.

MORDECAI: Esther, you must go to the king. You must ask him to save us.

210
 Old Testament

ESTHER: No one is allowed to come to the king unless he calls for us. If I go to him when he didn't ask for me, I could be killed.

MORDECAI: If you keep quiet now, we will be saved another way. But maybe you have become queen for this very reason!

ESTHER: All right. Ask all the Jews in **Susa** to fast with me for three days. Then I'll go to the king. If I die, I die.

NARRATOR: Three days later, Esther stood before the king, and he extended his scepter to her. She could come to him safely! She invited the king and Haman to a banquet. While they were eating, the king asked:

KING: Esther, what is your request? I'll give you anything you want.

ESTHER: I ask you for my life and for the lives of my people. Someone has plotted to kill us!

KING: Who would do such a thing?

ESTHER: This evil man Haman!

NARRATOR: The king left the room in a rage. When he returned, he saw Haman throwing himself down on Esther's couch to beg her mercy.

Fear

Esther left her house and family as a young woman. She had to keep her identity secret. Then she had to risk her life to stand before the king. There were many ways fear tried to stop Esther from entering her destiny. But she overcame fear—because others supported her.

KING: Will you attack the queen while I'm still here? Away with him!

ESTHER: Please save my people, too! Please write a law that will reverse the law Haman wrote!

KING: I give you and Mordecai my signet ring. Write whatever law you wish.

NARRATOR: Esther and Mordecai wrote a law saying the Jews could take the property of anyone who attacked them. What was meant to be a day of destruction was turned into a day of victory for the Jews!

ESTHER: All Jews for all generations should celebrate this day as Purim (named after the pur or lot). It will be a day of celebration. What our enemies meant for evil turned into a day of blessing for us!

Review It!

Who led the first group of people who returned to Judah? What important project did they build?

Which prophets encouraged them to finish building the temple? What did the prophets say?

What did Esther ask the Jews in Susa to do before she went to the king?

What evil thing did Haman plan for the Jews? What actually happened on that day?

Remember It!

SONG: *Ezra and Nehemiah, 12 Tribes* (second half)

Bonus! Minor Prophets Message verse 3

Learn the other six tribes.

- 12 Tribes (part 2)
- Gad
- Asshur
- Issacar
- Zebulun
- Benjamin
- Joseph (who had Ephraim and Manasseh)

Think About It!

Why did God want the temple rebuilt? Why couldn't people just worship him privately?

List the things that Esther may have feared. How did she overcome her fears? How do you think the group fast helped?

God took something meant for evil and turned it into a day of blessing. What does that mean for your life?

I am so special to God that he created something only I can do on earth.

Map It!

Dots show where cities are. Lines show where regions are. Label these places:

- Assyria
- Nineveh
- Damascus

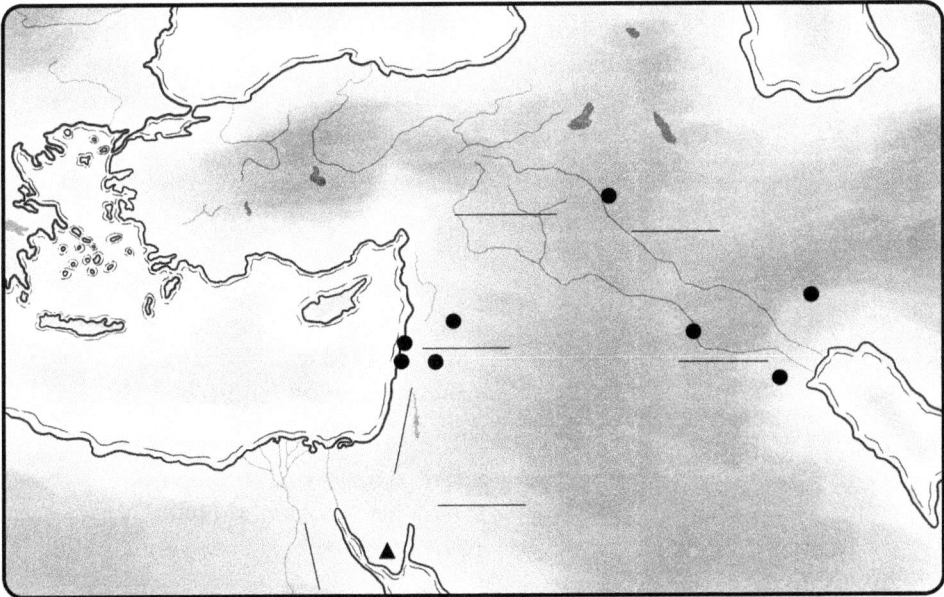

Answers in Appendix E Map 6

CHAPTER 36

The Return

Ezra, Nehemiah, Malachi

DIRECTIONS: Read the story to yourself. Or read it as a family with each person reading a different part aloud. When you come to a place name in **bold**, draw a wall in that location on a map in Appendix E.

Jerusalem's Wall is Rebuilt

Ezra 7-8, Nehemiah 1-4, 6, 8-12

NARRATOR: About 15 or 20 years after Esther saved her people, Ezra led another group of Jews to return to **Judah**. Ezra was a scribe descended from Aaron, the first high priest. A few thousand people returned with Ezra—mostly priests, Levites, and other people who served in the temple. They carried a lot of silver and gold donated by the king and others. Ezra gathered everyone together before their journey. He told them:

EZRA: I was embarrassed to ask the king for soldiers to protect us. I told him our God was very powerful. Now let's all fast and ask God to keep us safe on our trip to Jerusalem.

NARRATOR: God protected everyone on the long journey. When they arrived in Jerusalem, Ezra made sure the people were doing what God commanded. About ten years later, Nehemiah asked the king of Persia for permission to return to Jerusalem and rebuild the wall around the city. The king gave Nehemiah everything he asked for. He even made Nehemiah the governor of Judah.

NEHEMIAH: I knew our enemies wouldn't want me to rebuild the city wall. In the middle of the night, I rode all the way around the city, inspecting the broken wall. In the morning, I told people we must repair the wall.

PEOPLE: Let's start rebuilding right now!

NARRATOR: Each person repaired the part of the wall next to their house. Before long, Judah's enemies tried to stop their progress.

ENEMY: When they're not expecting it, we'll sneak in and attack them! That will put an end to their work!

NARRATOR: Nehemiah told the workers:

Worship

Israel was designed so everything would center around worship in the temple. It's a picture of how our lives work best, too. Everything we love and think about and do is designed to flow from a heart that is worshiping God.

NEHEMIAH: Don't be afraid of them! Remember how awesome the Lord is! I will station guards day and night. Half the men will work on the wall. The other half will carry weapons. We must be ready to fight at any moment!

NARRATOR: In just 52 days, the wall was completed!

NEHEMIAH: When our enemies saw how quickly we had built the wall, they were discouraged. They knew God had helped us do it.

NARRATOR: After the wall was complete, the people gathered in a plaza. They asked Ezra to read the law of Moses. From dawn till noon, Ezra read the law to the men, women, and children standing there. Ezra, Nehemiah, and the Levites who worked in the temple explained the law to the people. The next day the people discovered they were supposed to celebrate the Festival of Sukkot (Tents).

EZRA: Gather branches of olive, myrtle, palm, and other leafy trees. Make a temporary house like God commanded.

NARRATOR: With great joy, everyone set up shelters made from tree branches and lived in them. The Israelites hadn't kept this Festival since the days of Joshua. They celebrated together for one week.

NEHEMIAH: The leaders, the Levites, the priests, and I dedicated ourselves and the people to God. We agreed not to marry the neighboring people. They worship idols. We agreed to keep the Sabbath holy. We agreed to support the temple with our offerings and gifts.

NARRATOR: With Ezra the scribe, the people gained a deeper understanding of God's law. With Nehemiah the governor, the city grew more secure. Together these leaders turned the nation's heart back to God. They set in place a system that would support the temple and establish worship of the LORD in Israel.

Malachi Prophesies

Malachi 1-4

NARRATOR: Malachi prophesied after the return to Judah and after the temple was rebuilt. Scholars don't agree on whether he ministered before or during Ezra and Nehemiah's time in Jerusalem. Malachi spoke many of his messages as a conversation between God and the people of Israel.

GOD: I've loved you.

PEOPLE: How have you loved us?

GOD: I chose you as my own. Sons honor their father. Servants respect their master. If I am your father, where is my honor? If I am your master, where is my respect?

PEOPLE: How have we dishonored you?

GOD: You give me what is worthless, what you don't want yourselves! You offer blind and lame animals as a sacrifice to me. Try offering those animals to your governor. Would he show you favor?

MALACHI: The LORD's name will be honored everywhere, in all the nations. They will worship him from where the sun rises to where it sets.

PEOPLE: Why isn't God answering our prayers? We're crying and groaning to him. But he doesn't respond!

GOD: You have been unfaithful to the wife you married when you were young. I hate divorce. I hate violence. Be faithful. You are robbing me!

Whole Heart

The people followed the things God said to do. They brought him sacrifices. They worshiped at the temple. But God wanted honor, respect, service, and love. Who would be satisfied with someone who did the bare minimum, but felt no respect or love? God wanted their heart—all of it.

PEOPLE: How are we robbing you?

GOD: You're not bringing the full amount of money into the temple! Test me. Give me everything you should. Then see how I will open the windows of heaven and pour out a blessing on you until you don't have room for it all.

MALACHI: The people who honored the LORD spoke to each other. God noticed. A scroll was prepared, recording the names of all the people who respect God.

GOD: They will belong to me. I will spare them like a man spares the son who serves him. Then you'll see a difference between those who serve God and those who don't.

MALACHI: A day is coming where the LORD will burn the evil off of the people who are proud.

GOD: Remember the law of my servant Moses. I will send you Elijah the prophet before the great and terrible day of the LORD. He will encourage parents and children to return to me so I won't strike the earth to destroy it.

Review It!

Who returned with Ezra? What did Ezra do?

What building project did Nehemiah organize? How many days did it take to finish it?

What festival did the people keep after Ezra read them the law of Moses? What types of tree branches did they gather?

Name three things God wanted people to change, according to Malachi.

Remember It!

SONG: *Feasts*

Learn the feasts of the Jewish faith.

- Feasts
- Passover
- Unleavened Bread
- First Fruits
- Pentecost (or Shavuot)

- Trumpets (or Rosh Hashanah)
- Yom Kippur
- Sukkot (or Tents)

Think About It!

What part of Ezra and Nehemiah's work was the most important in your opinion? Why?

Listening to Malachi, how did God want people to treat him?

List three ways you can honor God with what he's given you, following the ideas of Malachi.

I am special to God. There is no one like me.

Map It!

Dots show where cities are. Lines show where regions are. Label these places:

- Tyre
- Sidon
- Hamath

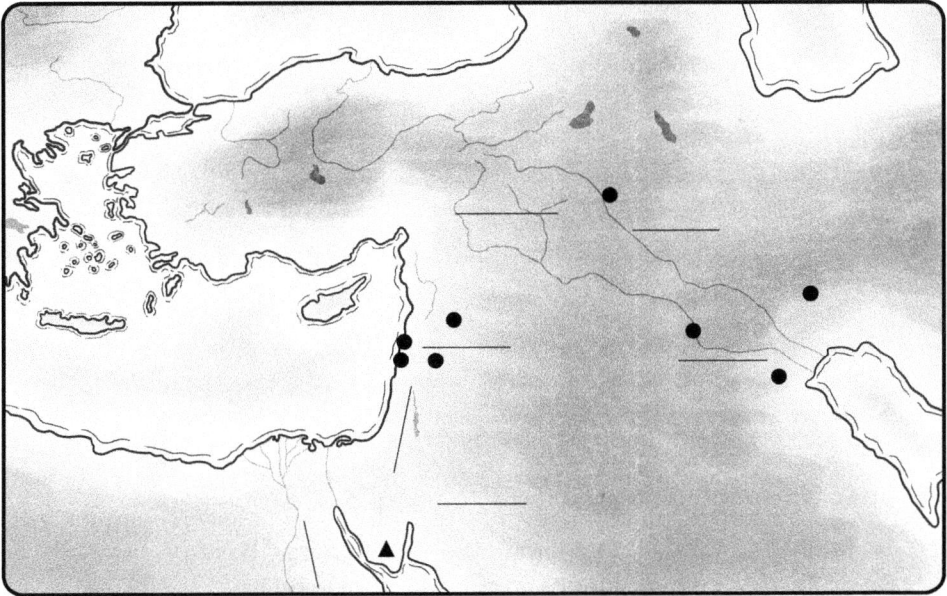

Answers in Appendix E Map 6

Key People in the Bible

Meet these most-mentioned people in the Bible.
You can learn their names with the songs that go with this book.

New Testament

12 Apostles

Of the hundreds that followed him, Jesus set aside 12 to be with him and to share his authority

SIMON PETER—Jesus changed his name from Simon to Peter (meaning "Rock"), spokesman of the apostles, always listed first among them, wrote two letters in the Bible, fisherman from Bethsaida living in Capernaum.

ANDREW—Peter's brother, fisherman, introduced Peter to Jesus.

JAMES—John's brother, nicknamed "Sons of Thunder" by Jesus, first apostle to die for his faith, fisherman from Capernaum.

JOHN—James' brother, nicknamed "Sons of Thunder" by Jesus, wrote about Jesus' life, three letters, and Revelation, only apostle to not die for his faith.

PHILIP—From Bethsaida, told his friend Nathaniel about Jesus.

BARTHOLOMEW—The Bible just lists him as an apostle. Some people think his nickname is Nathaniel.

THOMAS—Twin, wanted to touch Jesus' body before he believed he rose from death.

MATTHEW—Tax collector, wrote Matthew, from Capernaum.

JAMES SON OF ALPHAEUS—The Bible just lists him as an apostle.

THADDEUS (ALSO CALLED JUDAS THE SON OF JAMES)—He asked Jesus a question in John 14 about how Jesus was going to reveal himself to them.

SIMON THE ZEALOT—The Bible just lists him as an apostle. Many people think he either had belonged to a group who wanted political freedom or that he was zealous (very serious about) Moses' law.

JUDAS ISCARIOT—Kept the money bag for Jesus' ministry and stole from it, betrayed Jesus for 30 silver coins.

MATTHIAS—Replaced Judas Iscariot in Acts 1, followed Jesus for his entire ministry.

Jesus' Women Leaders

Many scholars believe these women were the leaders of Jesus' women disciples because more is said of them than of most of his other followers.

MARY MAGDALENE—Many scholars think she was the main leader of Jesus' women disciples, left everything to follow Jesus around, first to see Jesus raised from the dead, only person named in the Bible who was an eyewitness to Jesus' death, burial, and resurrection, seven demons cast from her, her name probably means Mary from Magdala (a city on the Sea of Galilee).

JOANNA—wife of King Herod's household manager, provided for Jesus out of her own resources, followed Jesus from town to town.

SUSANA—Provided for Jesus from her own resources, left everything to follow him from town to town.

MARY THE MOTHER OF JAMES AND JOSES—Eyewitness to Jesus' death, followed him and supported him.

MARY THE WIFE OF CLOPAS—Eyewitness to Jesus' death, followed him and supported him.

SALOME—Mother of apostles James and John, left everything to follow Jesus, begged Jesus to give her sons positions on his right and left in his kingdom, eyewitness to Jesus' death, one of the first to see Jesus risen from death.

People who Helped Spread the Good News

People mentioned 5 or more times in Acts and the Letters

PAUL—Acts follows three of his journeys to share about Jesus. Paul wrote many letters to churches.

BARNABAS—Joined Paul on his first journey, his real name was Joseph, from Cyprus, nicknamed Barnabas (meaning "son of encouragement") by the apostles.

TIMOTHY—Joined Paul on his second journey, leader in Ephesus later.

TITUS—Leader in Crete, part of Paul's team to share about Jesus.

JOHN MARK—Wrote Mark, cousin of Barnabas, joined Paul and Barnabas for the beginning of their first journey, helped Peter.

SILAS—Joined Paul on his second journey.

LUKE—Doctor who wrote Luke and Acts, joined Paul's team to travel and share about Jesus.

PRISCILLA AND AQUILA—Friends of Paul, taught Apollos about Jesus, tentmakers.

APOLLOS—Teacher and speaker, traveled to tell people about Jesus.

PETER—Apostle, wrote two letters in the Bible.

ARISTARCHUS—Joined Paul on his journey to Rome, from Thessalonica, part of Paul's team.

TYCHICUS—Joined Paul on part of his third journey, part of Paul's team, delivered letters to the Ephesians and Colossians.

Old Testament

Patriarchs and Matriarchs

The founders of the nation of Israel

ABRAHAM, SARAH, ISAAC, REBECCA, JACOB, LEAH, RACHEL

12 Tribes / 12 Sons of Jacob

Jacob's 12 sons who became the 12 tribes of Israel

REUBEN, SIMEON, LEVI, JUDAH, DAN, NAPHTALI, GAD, ASHUR, ISSACHAR, ZEBULUN, JOSEPH (WHO HAD EPHRAIM AND MANASSEH), BENJAMIN

Main Judges

Of the 12 judges, the 6 judges we're told the most about are:

OTHNIEL—Caleb's son-in-law who defeated Aram.

EHUD—Defeated Moab with his left hand.

DEBORAH—Defeated Canaan with the army commander Barak.

GIDEON—Defeated Midian with only 300 soldiers.

JEPHTHAH—Defeated Ammon.

SAMSON—Fought Philistia with super strength.

Kings of Judah

Kings who ruled over the united kingdom of Israel or over Judah

SAUL, DAVID, SOLOMON, REHOBOAM, ABIJAH, ASA, JEHOSHAPHAT, JEHORAM, AHAZIAH (ATHALIAH), JOASH, AMAZIAH, UZZIAH, JOTHAM, AHAZ, HEZEKIAH, MANASSEH, AMON, JOSIAH, JEHOAHAZ, JEHOIAKIM, JEHOICHIN, ZEDEKIAH

Kings of Israel

Kings who ruled over the northern kingdom called Israel

JEROBOAM, NADAB, BASHA, ELAH, ZIMRI, TIBNI, OMRI, AHAB, AHAZIAH, JORAM, JEHU, JEHOAHAZ, JEHOASH, JEROBOAM, ZECHARIAH, SHALLUM, MENAHEM, PEKAHIAH, PEKAH, HOSHEA

Major Prophets

Prophets who wrote longer books

ISAIAH—Prophet to Kings Ahaz and Hezekiah when nations attacked Jerusalem. Many prophecies about Jesus.

JEREMIAH—Prophet in Jerusalem before and during the fall to Babylon.

EZEKIEL—Prophet to the exiles in Babylon before and after the fall of Jerusalem.

DANIEL—Taken captive from Jerusalem, became a government official in Babylon. Had dreams about the kingdoms that would rule the Middle East.

Minor Prophets

The 12 prophets who wrote shorter books

AMOS—Judgment is coming unless people put away idols and treat the poor fairly.

HOSEA—Married an unfaithful wife to demonstrate how God felt when people prayed to idols.

JONAH—Swallowed by a fish before he agreed to preach to Nineveh.

OBADIAH—Edom will regret mistreating Jerusalem.

JOEL—When locusts ate everything, they revealed what the day of the LORD will be like. Fast and repent and maybe God will leave a blessing instead of judgment.

MICAH—Destruction is coming unless people put away idols and stop cheating people. Even if judgment comes, there will be a good ending.

NAHUM—Nineveh will be destroyed.

HABAKKUK—Talked to God about his plans to use Babylon to correct Judah.

ZEPHANIAH—Judgment is coming unless people put away idols and treat people fairly.

HAGGAI—Rebuild the temple and God will bless you.

ZECHARIAH—Eight visions in one night about God's plans to bless Jerusalem.

MALACHI—Honor God and worship him with a pure heart.

Other Key People

ADAM AND EVE—The first people God created.

NOAH—Built an ark to save the world.

MOSES—Led Israel out of slavery in Egypt.

JOSHUA—Led Israel into the land God promised to give them.

RUTH—King David's great-grandmother.

SAMUEL—First official prophet in Israel. He anointed the first two kings.

JOB—Righteous man who learned about God through suffering.

EZRA—Scribe, led people to return from Babylon to Judah, taught people the law of Moses.

NEHEMIAH—Governor of Judah who rebuilt the wall around Jerusalem.

ESTHER—Jewish queen of Persia who saved the Jews from a plot to kill them.

Appendix B

Key Events in the Bible (Timeline)

New Testament

1. Baptized by John the Baptist
2. Tempted in the Wilderness
3. First disciples follow him
4. Wedding in Cana—first Miracle
5. Cleanses the Temple
6. Tells Nicodemus how to see God's Kingdom
7. John the Baptist put in jail
8. Jesus moves to Capernaum
9. Jesus talks with a woman at a well
10. Jesus heals a nobleman's son
11. Jesus calls his disciples
12. Jesus preaches and heals throughout Galilee
13. Jesus heals a leper, disabled man, crippled, withered hand a more
14. Jesus picks 12 apostles
15. Many women Jesus healed follow him
16. Preaches a sermon on a mountain
17. Heals a soldier's servant
18. Raises a widow's son from the dead
19. Calms a storm
20. Casts out demons in Gadarenes
21. Heals a woman with a blood problem
22. Raises' Jairus' girl from the dead

23. Nazareth rejects him
24. Sends disciples out to preach and heal
25. Feeds 5,000
26. Walks on water
27. Heals a girl from Tyre area
28. Feeds 4,000
29. Peter says Jesus is God's Son
30. Jesus shines in glory
31. Jesus casts a demon from a boy
32. Jesus heals a man born blind
33. Jesus sends out 72 disciples
34. Jesus teaches at Mary and Martha's house
35. Jesus says he is One with God
36. Jesus heals dropsy on the Sabbath
37. Jesus raises Lazarus from the dead
38. Jesus heals 10 lepers
39. Jesus blesses children
40. Jesus teaches a rich young ruler
41. Jesus explains he will die and rise again
42. James and John ask for positions of power
43. Jesus heals blind Bartimaeus
44. Jesus eats with Zacchaeus
45. Jesus is crucified
46. Jesus' body is placed in a tomb
47. Jesus rises from the dead
48. Jesus Returns to Heaven
49. Holy Spirit comes at Pentecost
50. Peter and John heal a disabled man
51. Believers share everything in common and are persecuted
52. Philip preaches in Samaria
53. Philip baptizes an Ethiopian official

54. Saul persecutes the church
55. Gentiles believe in Jesus
56. Cyprus' Governor believes
57. In Pisidian Antioch Paul teaches in the synagogue
58. Paul does miracles in Iconium
59. Paul is stoned in Lystra
60. Silas and Timothy join Paul's Second Journey
61. Lydia believes
62. Paul and Silas are jailed in Philippi
63. Thessalonians and Bereans believe despite opposition
64. Paul preaches about the Unknown God in Athens
65. Paul spends a year and a half in Corinth
66. Paul sparks a revival then riot in Ephesus
67. Paul raises Eutychus from the dead
68. Agabus warns Paul about going to Jerusalem
69. Paul is arrested in the temple and spends two years in jail
70. Paul appeals to Caesar and is shipwrecked
71. Paul preaches in Rome
72. Apostles and their helpers write Letters
73. John writes Revelation

Old Testament

1. God creates everything
2. Adam and Eve sin
3. Flood
4. Tower of Babel
5. God chooses Abraham and Sarah to start a nation
6. Abraham and Sarah move to Canaan and God promises them the Land
7. Isaac, Rebecca, Jacob, Leah, and Rachel grow Abraham's Family
8. Israel moves to Egypt and becomes slaves
9. Moses leads Israel out of slavery
10. 10 commandments and the Law
11. The Tabernacle and the Feasts
12. Joshua leads Israel into Canaan
13. 12 Judges lead Israel
14. Samuel anoints the first two kings, Saul and David
15. God promises David an eternal dynasty
16. David and prophetic musicians write psalms
17. Solomon builds the Temple
18. Solomon writes wise books
19. Israel divides into two kingdoms—Israel and Judah
20. Jeroboam sets up idols in Israel
21. Asa's reforms in Judah
22. Ahab marries Jezebel who establishes Baal worship in Israel
23. Elijah confronts Baal's prophets on Mount Carmel
24. Jehoshaphat honors God but makes a bad alliance
25. Elijah and Elisha run schools to train prophets
26. Jehu removes Baal from Israel
27. Joash overthrows Athaliah's rule in Judah
28. Uzziah conquers and becomes proud

29. Jeroboam II extends Israel's territory but doesn't turn to God

30. Jonah, Amos, and Hosea prophesy in Israel

31. Israel falls to Assyria and is exiled

32. Isaiah, and Micah prophesy

33. Ahaz doesn't rely on God

34. God saves Jerusalem when Hezekiah prays

35. Manasseh acts wickedly then repents

36. Zephaniah, Habakkuk, and Jeremiah prophesy in Judah

37. Josiah's reforms

38. Daniel and Ezekiel are taken to Babylon

39. Judah falls to Babylon and is exiled

40. Temple is destroyed

41. Remnant returns and rebuilds the Temple

42. Haggai and Zechariah prophesy

43. Esther saves Jews in Persia

44. Ezra and Nehemiah return to Judah

45. Malachi prophesies

Research Behind the Book

How the Brain Learns Best

In the past fifty years, researchers have made giant leaps in understanding how God designed the brain to learn most efficiently. Using these principles, we can learn dramatically more with less effort. Unfortunately, few people have tried to apply these learning principles to studying the Bible—until now.

What Doesn't Work Well

One of the most surprising discoveries of learning research is how much we forget when all we do is read or listen to a message.[1] Most people can remember only about 10 percent of what they read or hear a few days later.[2] So just reading the Bible (and listening to sermons about it) is like taking the long, slow, uphill path to mastering the Bible's contents. If you only read the Bible, you'll forget most of what you examine. Any commentary, map, or chart you consult will be largely forgotten, too.

There is good news, though. Learning research has discovered how to dramatically increase what people remember—and understand—about what they read.

Making More Connections

Although people remember only about 10 percent of what they read or hear, by making connections through two or more media, recall can skyrocket to around 65 percent.[3] The old saying, "An illustration is worth ten thousand words" turns out to be literally true, as the title of a leading article in this field of research suggests.[4] Not only does recall increase, but understanding and application of the material can be around 70 to

80 percent better for people who are exposed to text and graphics as compared to people who just read text.[5] Learning researchers call this discovery "multi-media learning." By delivering information as text and graphics, learning becomes dramatically more efficient.

Another way to increase connections to the material is to make an "active response" to it. If learners do something—from typing in text to pushing a button to filling in blanks—as they read, retention and comprehension rates rise significantly. Some studies comparing reading a text to reading and making an "active response" to the text show a jump of 20 percent or more in both recall and practical application for those who perform "active responses."[6] Other studies show some learners do 90% better using active responding.[7]

How We Use these Breakthroughs

In *The Bible Unlocked*, we go beyond a "normal" Bible study. First, we become "active" learners drawing on maps (and writing in the book). Then we expose readers to multi-media learning by pairing the Bible lessons with maps—graphics that add depth to the information being studied. Next, the songs, games, and app activities build more connections in the brain to the material. These extra connections help process the Bible more deeply. They also engage more of the readers' senses. Both these things help boost recall, understanding, and application. Finally, by setting milestones, we help readers stick with their goals to achieve far greater results.

What Results Should You Expect?

Based on research into how the brain learns best, we should expect results like these:

- Kids should remember more of what they read in the Bible. Learning research suggests people should remember between 30% and 100% more when they study the Bible using *The Bible Unlocked* than they would by just reading the Bible, depending on what in the Bible they're studying.[8]

- Kids should learn Bible geography deeper and faster. Research suggests most people should see a 30% to 100% jump in retention of Bible geography.[9]

- Kids should understand and apply the Bible more deeply. By making more connections in the brain, we can process information on a deeper level. And we can apply that understanding to practical situations better. Studies show up to a nearly 80% leap in understanding and application using the methods we employ.[10]

- Kids should have more fun. The methods we use makes learning more fun, and learners are more likely to continue studying the material.[11] We believe exploring the Bible should be one of the most fun, life-upgrading experiences a reader could ever have.

This increase in understanding and application means readers can actually transform their lives more deeply by studying the Bible in this way.

---

1. John Medina, *Brain Rules* (Seattle, WA: Pear Press, 2008), 233-34 (summarizing research over the last forty-plus years).

2. Medina, 234 (people remember about 10 percent of what they hear after 72 hours); Richard E. Mayer, "The Promise of Multimedia Learning: Using the Same Instructional Design Methods across Different Media," *Learning and Instruction* 13, no. 2 (April 2003): 126 ("Our research shows, on average, students who listen to (or read) explanations that are presented solely as words are unable to remember most of the key ideas and experience difficulty in using what was presented to solve new problems.").

3. Medina, 234. Numerous studies report an increased recall, in varying degrees, when learners view graphics in addition to reading or hearing text. See Peter S. Hous, et al., "The Role of Pictures in Improving Health Communication: A Review of Research on Attention, Comprehension, Recall, and Adherence," *Patient Education and Counseling* 61 (2006): 184 (authors reviewed 216 references discussing research into "pictures and recall," "almost all of which reported that written or spoken text plus pictures are better remembered than just text alone.").

4. Richard E. Mayer and Joan K. Gallini, "When is an Illustration Worth Ten Thousand Words?" *Journal of Educational Psychology* 82, vol. 4 (December 1990): 715-726.

5. Mayer, "The Promise of Multimedia Learning," 132-34 (finding a median of 68% and 78% "more creative solutions to problem-solving questions" for multi-media learners in two studies comparing reading text to reading text and viewing graphics in a "book-based environment").

6. Roger M. Tudor, "Isolating the Effects of Active Responding in Computer-Based Instruction," *Journal of Applied Behavioral Analysis* 28, no. 3 (Fall 1995): 343-344 (finding that students who engaged in active responses while reading remembered 22.5% more material than students who just read the material); see also Fernando Armendariz and

John Umbreit, "Using Active Responding to Reduce Disruptive Behavior in a General Education Classroom," *Journal of Positive Behavior Interventions* 1, no. 3 (Summer 1999): 152 (scores increased by 20% when using active responding); Tudor, R. M. and Bostow, D.E., "Computer- Programmed Instruction: The relation of Required Interaction to Practical Application," *Journal of Applied Behavioral Analysis* 24 (1991): 361-368 (finding that students who engaged in active responses while reading remembered 13% more and applied that knowledge 21% better than students who just read the material); Nancy A. Neef, Brandon E. McCord and Summer J. Ferreri, "Effects of Guided Notes Verses Completed Notes during Lectures on College Students' Quiz Performance," *Journal of Applied Behavioral Analysis* 39, vol. 1 (Spring 2006): 129 (students engaged in active responding while reading scored 27% better on analysis questions than students who only read material).

7. Malanga and William J. Sweeney, "Increasing Active Student Responding in a University Applied Behavior Analysis Course: The Effect of Daily Assessment and Response Cards on End of Week Quiz Scores," *Journal of Behavioral Education* 17, no. 2 (June 2008).

8. Tudor, 343-344; Armenariz and Umbreit, 152; Tudor and Boston, 361-368; Need, McCord, and Ferrari, 129; Malanga and Sweeney.

9. Ibid.

10. Mayer, 127, 131, 134.

11. E.g., Jennifer Archer, "Achievement Goals as a Measure of Motivation in University Students," *Contemporary Educational Psychology* 19 (1994): 442 (setting mastery goals motivates learners and makes learning more fun).

Diagrams and Charts

Tabernacle

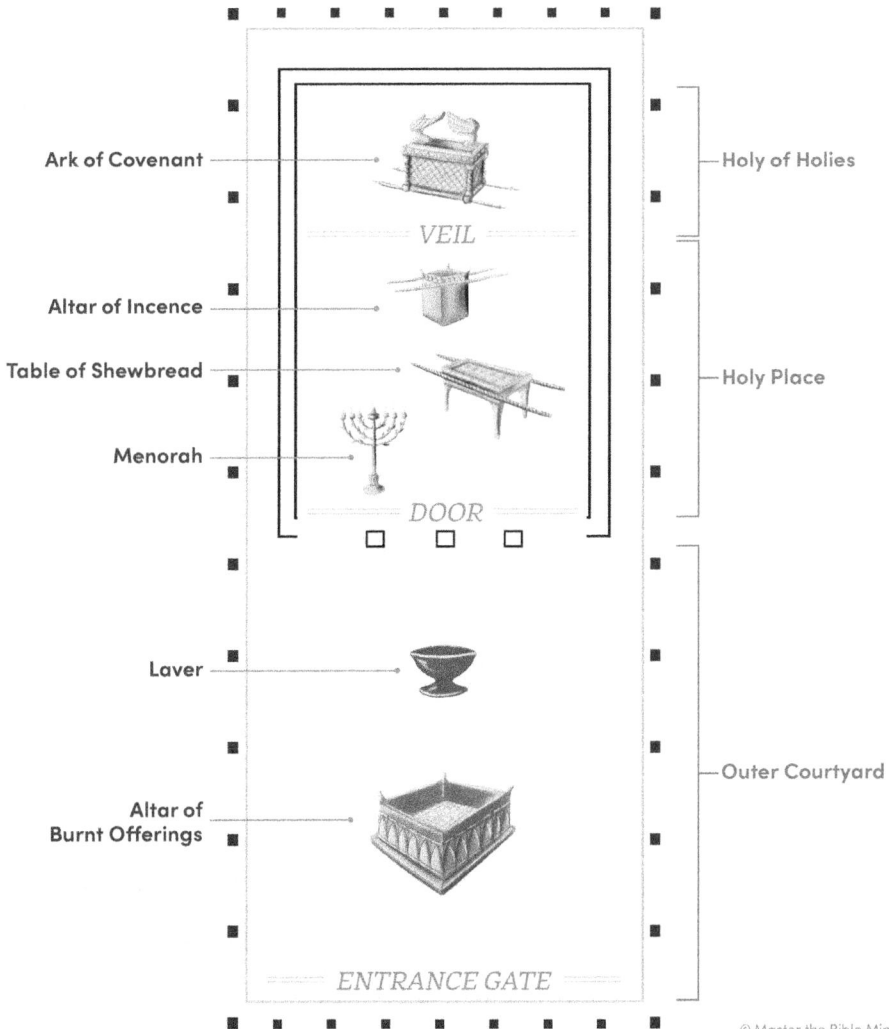

Ark of Covenant — Holy of Holies

VEIL

Altar of Incence

Table of Shewbread — Holy Place

Menorah

DOOR

Laver

Outer Courtyard

Altar of Burnt Offerings

ENTRANCE GATE

Bible Festivals

	FESTIVAL	POINTS TO WHEN...	BIBLE
SPRING FESTIVALS First time Jesus comes	Passover	Jesus dies.	Ex. 12:1-36; Lev. 23:4-5; Num. 28:16; Matt. 26:17-30; Mark 14:12-26; Luke 22:7-23; John 13
	Unleavened Bread	Jesus is buried.	Lev. 23:6-8; Num. 28:17-25; Matt. 27:57-61; John 19:38-42; 1 Cor. 5:7-8
	First Fruits	Jesus rises from death.	Lev. 23:9-14; John 20:1; 1 Cor. 15:20; Rom. 11:16
	Shavuot (Pentecost)	Holy Spirit lives in Jesus' followers.	Exodus 34:22-23; Lev 23:15-21; Num. 28:26-31; Deut. 16:10-12; Acts 2

	FESTIVAL	POINTS TO WHEN...	BIBLE
FALL FESTIVALS Second time Jesus comes	Trumpets (Rosh Hosannah, Bible New Years)	Trumpet is blown to... • tell us judgment is beginning • resurrect dead • celebrate Jesus' wedding • announce Jesus is king	Lev. 23:24-25; Num. 29:1-6; 1 Cor. 15:51-54; 1 Thes. 4:13-18; Rev. 20:11-12
	Yom Kippur (Day of Atonement)	Jesus returns and judges the world.	Lev. 16:1-24; Lev. 23:26-32; Num. 29:7-11; Heb. 9:1-14; Zech 12:1-10; Matt. 24:29-31; Rev. 1:7, Rev. 19:11-16; Rev. 11:18-19; Acts 24:9
	Sukkoth (Tents)	Jesus lives with his people forever.	Lev. 23:33-34; Num. 29:12-40; Zech. 14:4-21; Rev. 22:1-5

Maps

Map 1: Most-Mentioned Places in the New Testament Holy Land

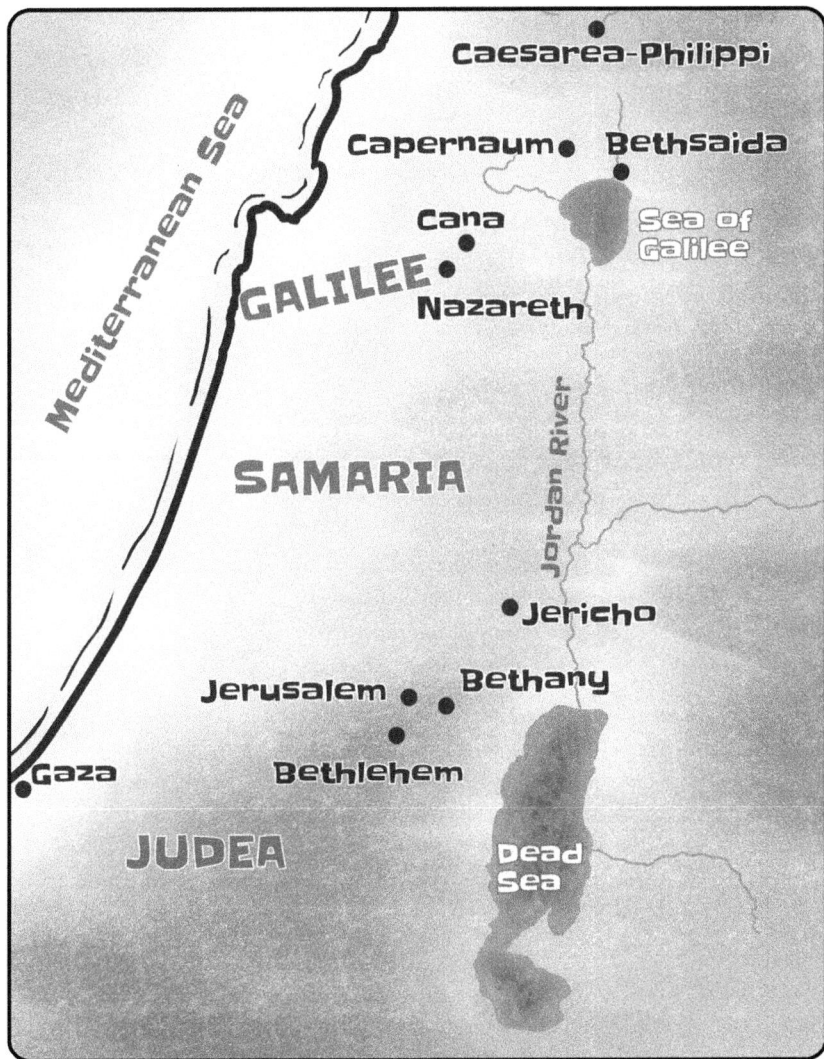

Map 2: Most-Mentioned Places in the New Testament Roman World

Rome • Macedonia • Philippi • Thessalonica • Berea • Greece • Athens • Corinth • Troas • Asia • Ephesus • Colossae • Crete • Galatia • Antioch in Pisidia • Iconium • Lystra • Derbe • Cilicia • Antioch • Cyprus • Syria • Damascus • Caesarea • Jerusalem

© Master the Bible Ministries

Map 3: Most-Mentioned Places in the Old Testament Holy Land

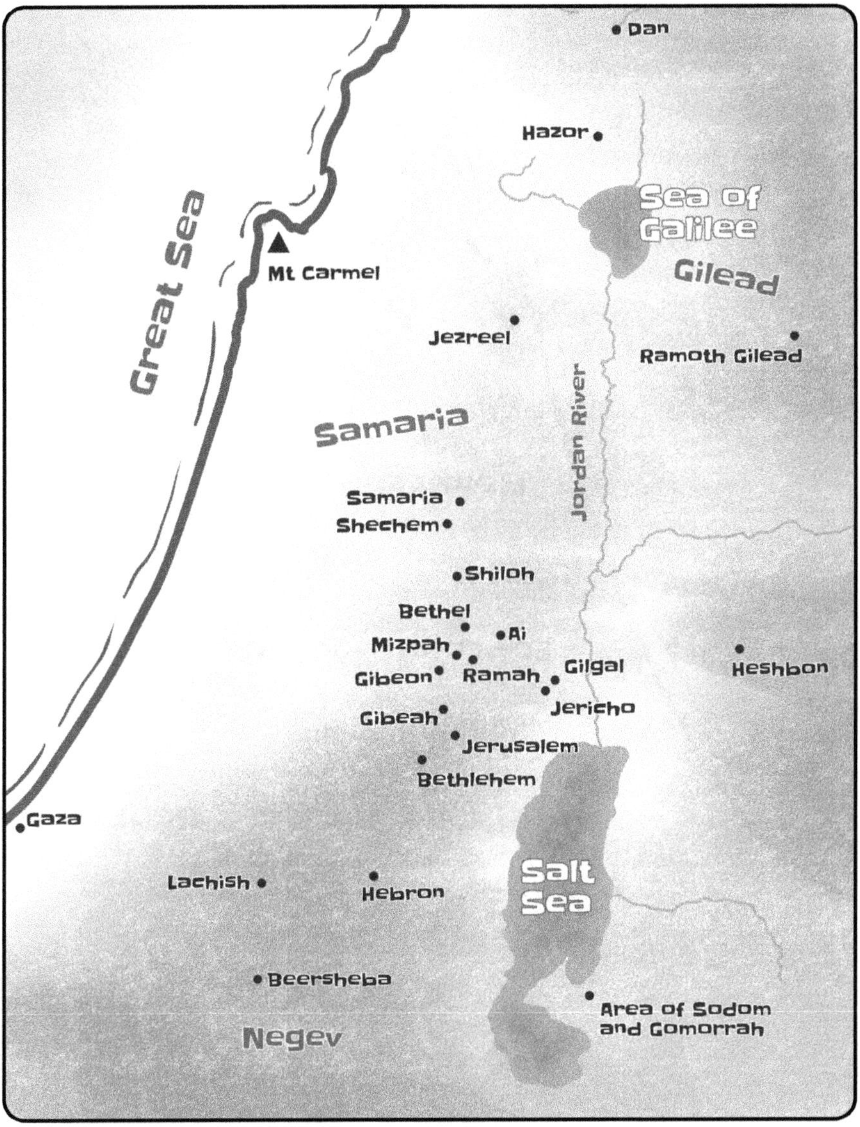
Dan
Hazor
Sea of Galilee
Gilead
Great Sea
Mt Carmel
Jezreel
Ramoth Gilead
Jordan River
Samaria
Samaria
Shechem
Shiloh
Bethel
Ai
Mizpah
Gibeon
Ramah
Gilgal
Heshbon
Jericho
Gibeah
Jerusalem
Bethlehem
Gaza
Lachish
Hebron
Salt Sea
Beersheba
Area of Sodom and Gomorrah
Negev

© Master the Bible Ministries

Map 4: Old Testament Tribes

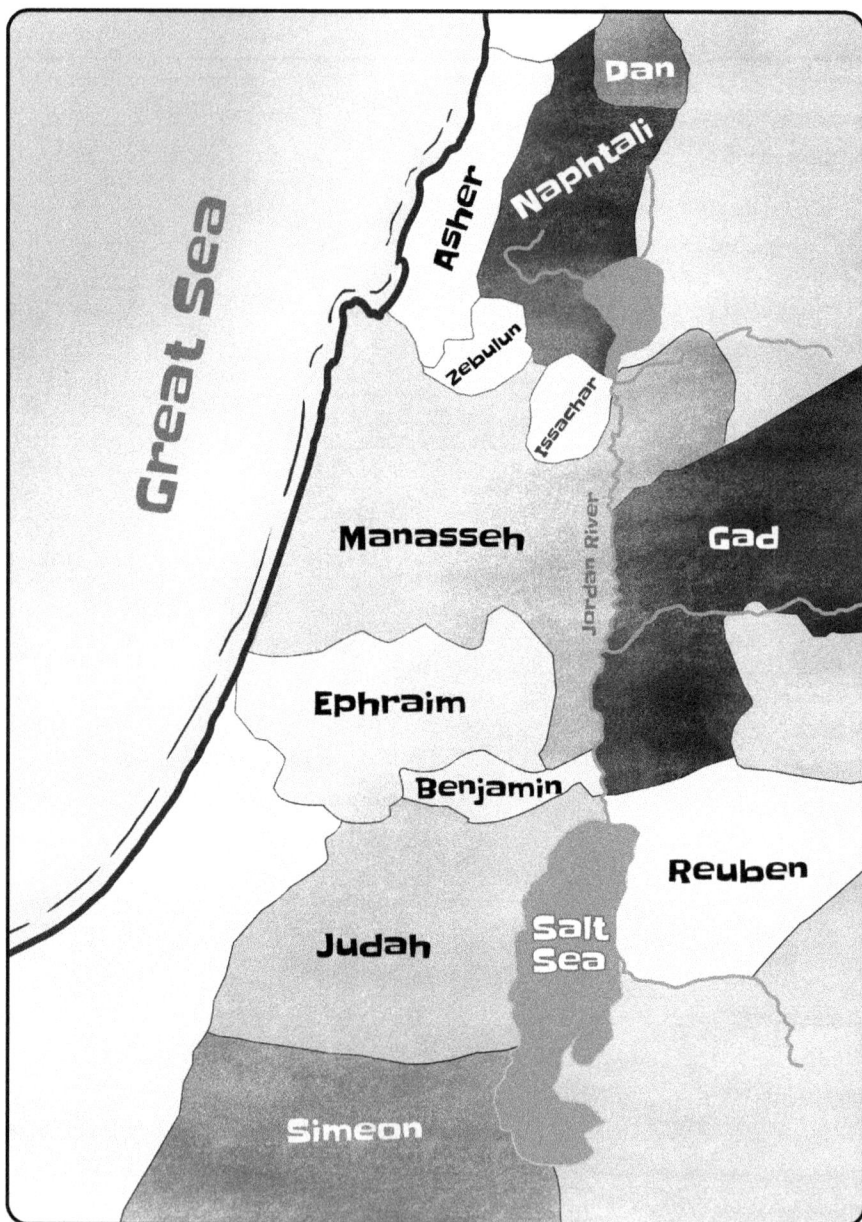

Great Sea

Dan

Naphtali

Asher

Zebulun

Issachar

Jordan River

Manasseh

Gad

Ephraim

Benjamin

Reuben

Judah

Salt Sea

Simeon

© Master the Bible Ministries

Map 5: Most-Mentioned Surrounding Nations in the Old Testament

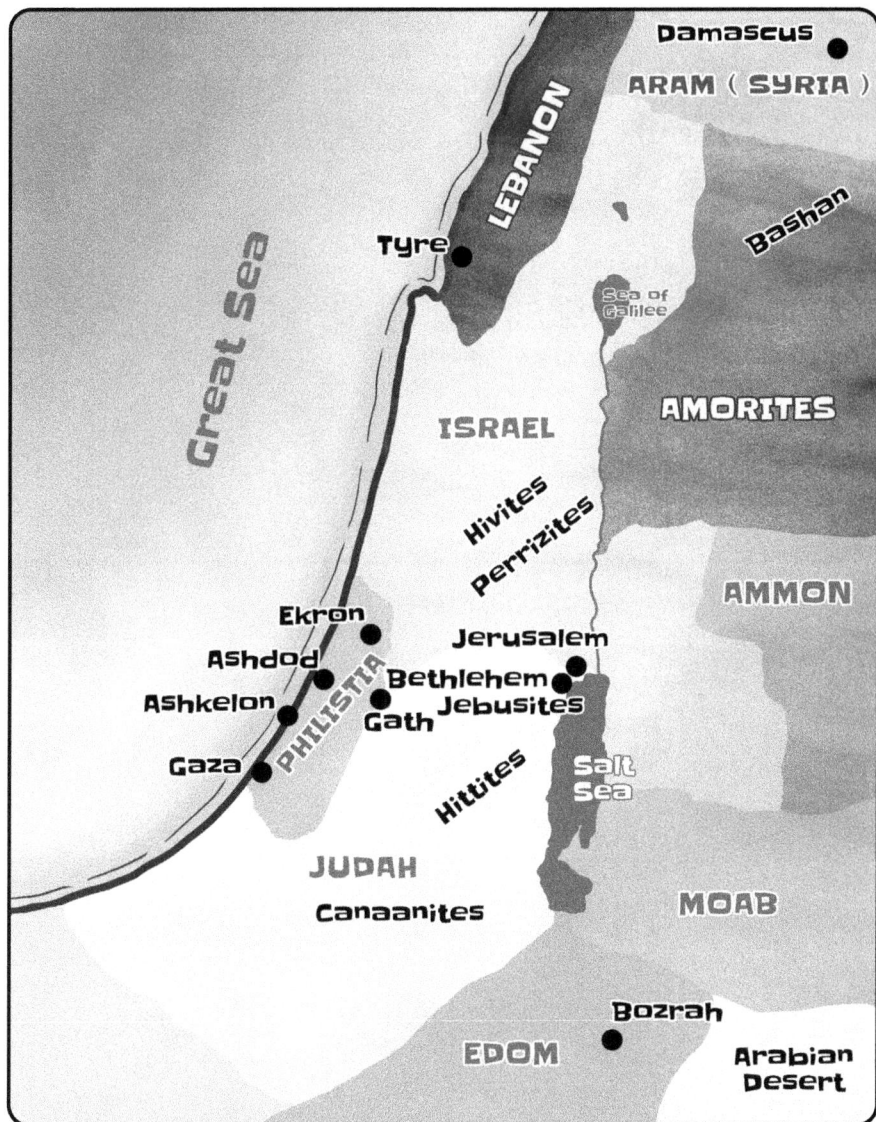

Damascus

ARAM (SYRIA)

LEBANON

Bashan

Great Sea

Tyre

Sea of Galilee

ISRAEL

AMORITES

Hivites

Perrizites

AMMON

Ekron

Ashdod

Jerusalem

Ashkelon

Bethlehem

PHILISTIA

Jebusites

Gath

Gaza

Hittites

Salt Sea

JUDAH

Canaanites

MOAB

Bozrah

EDOM

Arabian Desert

© Master the Bible Ministries

Map 6: Most-Mentioned Places in the Middle East

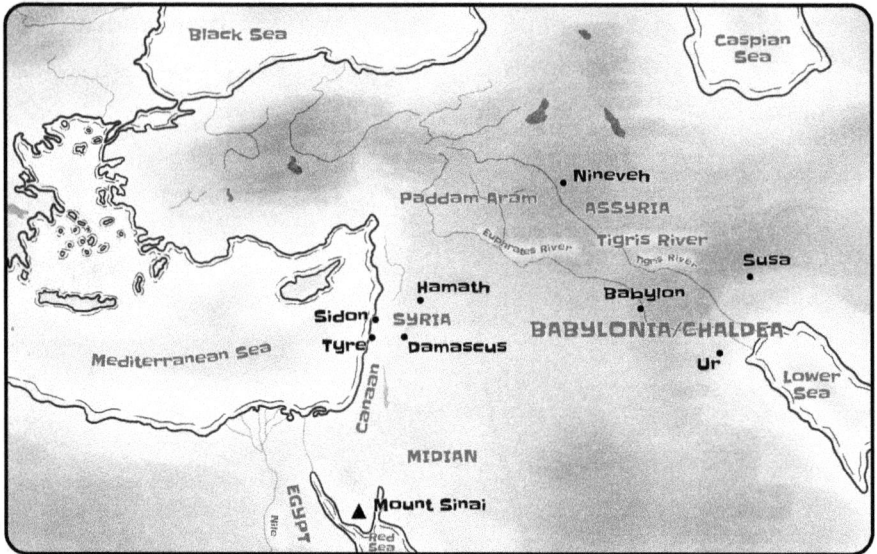

www.ingramcontent.com/pod-product-compliance
Lightning Source LLC
Chambersburg PA
CBHW061818040426
42447CB00012B/2714